TERRY PRATCHETT

WRITERS AND THEIR WORK

SERIES EDITORS:

Professor Dinah Birch CBE,
University of Liverpool
Professor Dame Janet Beer,
University of Liverpool

Writers and Their Work, launched in 1994 in association with the British Council, won immediate acclaim for its publication of brief but rigorous critical examinations of the works of distinguished writers and schools of writing. The series embraces the best of modern literary theory and criticism, and features studies of many popular contemporary writers, as well as the canonical figures of literature and important literary genres.

First published in 2026 by
Liverpool University Press
4 Cambridge Street
Liverpool L69 7ZU

British Library Cataloguing-in-Publication Data
A catalogue record for this book is available from the British Library

ISBN 978-1-80596-688-3 (hardback)
ISBN 978-1-80596-721-7 (paperback)

Typeset by Carnegie Book Production, Lancaster
Printed and bound by CPI Group (UK) Ltd, Croydon CR0 4YY

TERRY PRATCHETT

Andy Sawyer

To Marion Sawyer, who always wanted to see books with my name on, and to Mary Sawyer, who has to put up with me trying to write them.

Contents

Preface

Terry Pratchett wrote over fifty books – many more if collaborations and authorised Discworld spin-offs, and collections of children's stories reprinted after his death are included. In a short survey of his work, it would be impossible to cover each book at length. The reader is therefore directed elsewhere for full examination – to the books themselves, of course; to internet fan sites such as www.lspace.org; the growing corpus of books and articles about Pratchett; and especially to the website maintained by his former agent, Colin Smythe, at https://colinsmythe.co.uk/. Much critical attention is devoted to his successful Discworld series and to his equally successful (and award-winning) novels for children. In this book, I have tried to present the wide range, development, and thematic complexity of a writer who, in the phrase he used in the back-cover blurbs of several novels, was 'occasionally […] accused of literature'.

Beginning with a brief survey of his life and chapters on his early works, the development of Discworld and the non-Discworld novels, I have continued with chapters drawing more widely from his works showing the importance of story and storytelling for an appreciation of his fiction. I have examined how he shows that the narratives we build about ourselves and the world can be both shackling and liberating, how he draws upon and plays with the conventions and thematics of genre, and how his maturity and expertise as a writer allowed him to outgrow the pastiche and parody of his earlier works without dismissing the capability of fantasy and science fiction to foreground morality and ethics. I conclude with a return to some of the items in the first chapter to discuss his relationship with his audience, or rather, his various audiences.

Acknowledgements

Although they have not (as yet) seen the text, I am grateful for the support of Colin Smythe (Terry Pratchett's former agent) when I was the librarian in charge of the Science Fiction Foundation Collection in Special Collections, University of Liverpool Library, and for the kind dedication to 'A Librarian who likes to say "Oook" (but in a nice way)' in Andrew M. Butler's *An Unofficial Companion to the Novels of Terry Pratchett*. Grateful thanks are due to the University of Liverpool Library, especially Inter-Library Loans and my former colleagues in Special Collections and Archives for putting up with me as a 'customer'. Thanks are also due to Christabel Scaife of Liverpool University Press, the anonymous reviewers whose encouraging reports helped me focus upon the book's structure, and above all to Mary Sawyer, who kept me glued to the task while trying not to look *too* disbelieving at the words 'almost finished'.

Biographical Outline

Note: This outline is selective and does not contain most of the spin-off/related material – the games, revised reprints, dramatic performances, adaptations, artefacts, appearances or events associated with Terry Pratchett and the Discworld series. For fuller information, the reader is directed to the extensive website maintained by Pratchett's former agent Colin Smythe at https://colinsmythe.co.uk/terry-pratchett/ and the biography by his literary executor Rob Wilkins, *Terry Pratchett, A Life with Footnotes* (Doubleday, 2022).

1948	Born 28 April, Beaconsfield, Buckinghamshire.
1953	Attended Holtspur Primary School, Beaconsfield.
1959	Attended High Wycombe Technical High School, Buckinghamshire.
1960	Unofficial 'Saturday boy' job, Beaconsfield Library.
1963	'The Hades Business' published, *Science Fantasy* magazine, vol. 20, no. 60.
1964	Attends RePetercon (Easter Science Fiction Convention), Peterborough.
1965	Attends Brumcon II (Easter Science Fiction Convention), Birmingham and Loncon II (23rd World Science Fiction Convention, London).
	Leaves school to become trainee reporter on *Bucks Free Press*.
	'Night Dweller' published, *New Worlds*, vol. 49, no. 156.
1968	Marries Lyn Purves.
1970	News reporter, *Western Daily Press*, Bristol.
1971	Publication of first novel, *The Carpet People* (Colin Smythe Ltd.).

1972	Sub-editor at *Bucks Free Press*.
1973	Sub-editor at *Bath & Wilts Evening Chronicle*.
1976	Publication of *Dark Side of the Sun*.
	Birth of daughter Rhianna.
1979	Publicity Officer for Central Electricity Generating Board (CEGB).
1981	*Strata*.
1983	*The Colour of Magic* (1st Discworld novel).
1985	*The Colour of Magic* serialised, BBC Radio 4 *Woman's Hour*, following Corgi paperback publication.
1986	*The Light Fantastic* (2nd Discworld novel).
1987	*Equal Rites* (3rd Discworld novel); serialised, BBC Radio 4's *Woman's Hour*.
	Colin Smythe becomes Pratchett's literary agent.
	Mort (4th Discworld novel).
1988	*Sourcery* (5th Discworld novel).
	Wyrd Sisters (6th Discworld novel).
1989	*Pyramids* (7th Discworld novel).
	Truckers (1st of Bromeliad Trilogy).
	The Unadulterated Cat, illus. Gray Jolliffe.
	Guards! Guards! (8th Discworld novel).
1990	*Diggers* (2nd of Bromeliad Trilogy).
	Good Omens (with Neil Gaiman).
	Eric (9th Discworld novel).
	Wings (3rd of Bromeliad Trilogy).
	Moving Pictures (10th Discworld novel).
1991	*Reaper Man* (11th Discworld novel).
	Witches Abroad (12th Discworld novel).
1992	Thames TV broadcast 13-part serial of *Truckers*.
	Small Gods (13th Discworld novel).
	Revised version of *The Carpet People*.
	Only You Can Save Mankind (1st Johnny Maxwell novel).
	Lords and Ladies (14th Discworld novel).
1993	*Johnny and the Dead* (2nd Johnny Maxwell novel).
	Men at Arms (15th Discworld novel).
	The Streets of Ankh-Morpork, map, with Stephen Player (Corgi); first of a series of Discworld-related maps.
1994	Chairman of Society of Authors (1994–1995).
	Soul Music (16th Discworld novel).

	Interesting Times (17th Discworld novel).
	The Discworld Companion (with Stephen Briggs) – reprinted and enlarged through several editions.
1995	*Maskerade* (18th Discworld novel).
1996	BBC Radio 4 three-part adaptation of *Only You Can Save Mankind*.
	Johnny and the Bomb (3rd Johnny Maxwell novel); wins Smarties Prize Silver Award.
	Play-texts of *Mort* and *Wyrd Sisters*, by Stephen Briggs; first of a series of adaptations following successful amateur productions.
	Feet of Clay (19th Discworld novel).
	Hogfather (20th Discworld novel).
	1st International Discworld Convention, Manchester. First of a series of fan-organised conventions in the UK, Australia, Germany, USA, Poland and elsewhere.
1997	Channel 4 animated adaptation of *Wyrd Sisters* broadcast.
	Discworld's Unseen University Diary for 1998 (with Stephen Briggs); the first of a series of themed diaries and almanacs.
	Jingo (21st Discworld novel).
1998	Awarded OBE for Services to Literature.
	The Last Continent (22nd Discworld novel).
	Carpe Jugulum (23rd Discworld novel).
	Channel 4 adaptation of *Soul Music*.
1999	Honorary D.Litt., University of Warwick.
	The Science of Discworld with Ian Stewart and Jack Cohen.
	Discworld Collector's Edition 1999 Calendar: first of a series of calendars illustrated by Josh Kirby, Paul Kidby, Marc Simonetti and others.
	The Fifth Elephant (24th Discworld novel).
	Nanny Ogg's Cookbook (Doubleday).
2000	*Terry Pratchett: Guilty of Literature,* eds Andrew M. Butler, Edward James and Farah Mendlesohn (Science Fiction Foundation).
	The Truth (25th Discworld novel).
2001	*Thief of Time* (26th Discworld novel).
	Honorary D.Litt., University of Portsmouth.

The Last Hero, illus. Paul Kidby (27th Discworld novel).

The Amazing Maurice and His Educated Rodents (28th Discworld novel); receives Carnegie Award for best children's book of the year.

2002 *The Science of Discworld II: The Globe* with Ian Stewart and Jack Cohen.

Night Watch (29th Discworld novel); receives Prometheus Award, from the Libertarian Futurist Society).

2003 *The Wee Free Men* (30th Discworld novel); receives 2004 *Locus* award for Best Young Adult Novel of 2003, Teen Choice W.H. Smith Book Award for 2004.

Monstrous Regiment (31st Discworld novel).

23 August: BBC Radio 4 adaptation of *The Amazing Maurice*.

Honorary D.Litt., University of Bath.

2004 *A Hat Full of Sky* (32nd Discworld novel) receives 2005 *Locus* award for Best Young Adult Novel of 2004.

Once More With Footnotes (collected shorter fiction and non-fiction) (NESFA Press).

The Art of Discworld (text, Terry Pratchett; Art, Paul Kidby).

Going Postal (33rd Discworld novel).

BBC Radio 4 four-part adaptation of *Mort*.

Guest of Honour Noreascon 4 (62nd World Science Fiction Convention).

Honorary D.Litt., Bristol University.

2005 BBC Radio 4 four-part adaptation of *Mort*.

The Science of Discworld III: Darwin's Watch with Ian Stewart and Jack Cohen.

Thud! (34th Discworld novel).

Where's My Cow? illus. Melvyn Grant.

2006 *Wintersmith* (35th Discworld novel) receives 2007 Locus Award for Best Young Adult novel of 2006).

BBC Radio 4 four-part adaptation of *Small Gods*.

Sky TV two-part adaptation of *Hogfather*.

2007 *Making Money* (36th Discworld novel), receives Locus Best Fantasy Novel Award.

	The Wit and Wisdom of Discworld (with Stephen Briggs).
	Diagnosed with early-onset Alzheimer's disease.
2008	BBC Radio 4 five-part adaptation of *Night Watch*.
	Sky TV two-part adaptation of *The Colour of Magic/ The Light Fantastic*.
	Nation.
	The Folklore of Discworld (with Jacqueline Simpson).
	Donates $1,000,000 to Alzheimer's Research Trust.
	Honorary D.Litt., Buckinghamshire New University.
	Honorary D.Litt., Trinity College Dublin.
2009	*Unseen Academicals* (37th Discworld novel).
	Honorary D.Litt., Bradford University.
	Honorary D.Litt., Winchester University.
	Knighted in New Year Honours List for services to literature.
2010	*I Shall Wear Midnight* (38th Discworld novel).
	BBC Radio 7 eight-part reading of *Nation*.
	Sky TV *Going Postal* adaptation.
	Delivers BBC Richard Dimbleby Lecture, 'Shaking Hands with Death'.
	Inaugural lecture as Adjunct Professor, Trinity College Dublin.
	World Fantasy Convention Award for Life Achievement.
	National Book Awards Outstanding Achievement award (tie with Martin Amis).
2011	*Snuff* (39th Discworld novel), awarded Bollinger Everyman P. G. Wodehouse Award for comic literature.
	BBC2 broadcast of documentary *Terry Pratchett: Choosing to Die* (Scottish BAFTA Best Documentary Award, British BAFTA, Royal Television Society's Best Documentary Award, Grierson Award, International Emmy).
	Awarded Karl Edward Wagner Special Award by British Fantasy Society.
	American Library Association's Margaret A. Edwards award for 'significant and lasting contribution to young adult literature'.

	Appointed Honorary Fellow, University College London (after working with researchers at UCL following his diagnosis).
2012	*Miss Felicity Beedle's 'The World of Poo'* (with Bernard and Isobel Pearson). *The Long Earth* (with Stephen Baxter). *Dodger.* *A Blink of the Screen* (collected short fiction).
2013	*The Science of Discworld IV: Judgement Day* (with Ian Stewart and Jack Cohen). *The Long War* (with Stephen Baxter). *Raising Steam* (40th Discworld novel). *Dodger's Guide to London.* BBC Radio 4 four-part adaptation of *Eric*. Honorary D.Litt., Open University.
2014	*The Long Mars* (with Stephen Baxter). *Dragons at Crumbling Castle.* *A Slip of the Keyboard* (collected non-fiction). Honorary D.Litt., University of South Australia.
2015	Died 12 March from the effects of posterior cortical atrophy. 25 March: humanist funeral at Salisbury Crematorium. *The Shepherd's Crown* (41st Discworld novel). *The Long Utopia* (with Stephen Baxter).
2016	*The Long Cosmos* (with Stephen Baxter). *The Witch's Vacuum Cleaner.*
2017	*Father Christmas's Fake Beard.*
2020	*The Time-Travelling Caveman.*
2023	*A Stroke of the Pen: The Lost Stories.*
2025	*Tales of Wizards and Dragons.*

Abbreviations

Terry Pratchett books are available in numerous editions, not only hardback, paperback and ebook, but omnibus, commemorative and collector's editions.

Citations in the text are to the first editions.

ABOTS	A Blink on the Screen
AM	The Amazing Maurice and His Educated Rodents
ASOTK	A Slip of the Keyboard
CJ	Carpe Jugulum
COM	The Colour of Magic
CP1	The Carpet People (1971)
CP2	The Carpet People (1992 rev. ed.)
Di	Diggers
Do	Dodger
DSOTS	The Dark Side of the Sun
E	Eric
ER	Equal Rites
FE	The Fifth Elephant
FOC	Feet of Clay
GG	Guards! Guards!
GO	Good Omens
GP	Going Postal
H	Hogfather
HFOS	A Hat Full of Sky
ISWM	I Shall Wear Midnight
IT	Interesting Times
J	Jingo
JANT	Johnny and the Dead
JATB	Johnny and the Bomb

1

Introduction

In 1994, a BBC2 *Late Review* discussion on Terry Pratchett as one of the literary sensations of recent years began by asking whether his readers were 'stupid'.

To a flurry of sniggers, poet and critic Tom Paulin compared reading a Pratchett novel to 'picking up a stone. You see all these insects scurrying around and you think what on Earth are they up to?'. Newspaper columnist Allison Pearson joined in, claiming 'I got to about page 151 and I actually wrote across the centre of the page, you know, "I just can't go on [...] I would be surprised if any women wanted to read these books"'. Paulin dismissed Pratchett as 'a complete amateur! Doesn't even write in chapters!'.[1]

Pratchett fans took great delight in noting that Paulin's poems did not even rhyme and that the career of this 'Boys' Own stuff' writer took off after the third Discworld novel – *Equal Rites* – was serialised on BBC Radio 4's *Woman's Hour* in 1987. But while Pratchett's personal assistant and biographer Rob Wilkins put the apparent hostility towards Pratchett down to 'generally unpleasant ignorance masquerading as informed reaction',[2] there was perhaps more going on. The interesting thing about the scorn of the 'Late Reviewers', directed at what they obviously considered a soft target, was that Pratchett was without a university background, a working-class writer, a comedy writer, a *fantasy* writer; one who 'cultivated a sincere and mutually respectful relationship with his readers'.[3] As Pratchett himself put it in a *Daily Telegraph* interview with Boris Johnson some years later, '[w]riting is a collaborative process. It's not until it's ended up in someone's head that it exists'.[4] It is difficult not to discern a sense of bafflement, even resentment, that here there was a successful writer who had achieved mass popularity by

1

employing such 'low' techniques as fantasy and humour, and that this resentment was coupled with unwillingness to look at what he was doing and *how* he was doing it. Boris Johnson's interview, although genial, still talks of 'this stuff', 'nerds' and 'whimsy', and ends with a confession that Pratchett's success is beyond him.

At that stage of his life, Pratchett was a highly successful writer. *Interesting Times*, published in November 1994, was the seventeenth Discworld novel, and he had already published successful novels for children. He was chairman of the Society of Authors. He was, above all, a *working* writer, having sold his first professional story at the age of sixteen, while still at school, and eschewing the path of A' levels and university to develop his craft as a journalist on local newspapers. A voracious reader, he had used his unofficial Saturday job at Beaconsfield library to encounter a range of reading material which gave him an education ranging far beyond that of most university courses, and his attendance at science fiction conventions enabled him to mix with writers and readers in a way 'literary' writers, at 'book festivals', generally didn't.

This gave him a core readership which rapidly developed from sf fans to a wider, if not necessarily better-read, audience. Women who listened to *Equal Rites* (the first Discworld novel – *The Colour of Magic* – had also been serialised in 1985) and librarians who applauded his championing of the profession became factors in the growth of his popularity. In a lecture delivered in 1999 he was still referring to himself as a journalist trained by working journalists, 'in contrast to the other sort, who go straight from university into a column on an upmarket daily [...] where they can primp and posture in their little play street without being knocked down by real life'.[5] It is tempting to note, in that 'in contrast to the other sort', not only a testy response to the supercilious bafflement which greeted his popularity, but also wariness about 'academic' standards from someone who, at primary school, was branded 'one of the losers' but who nevertheless passed for grammar school thanks to his natural high intelligence and his capacity for hard work.[6]

As his career developed, however, members of the 'literary establishment' recognised his gifts. Introducing a collection of Pratchett's short fiction (*A Blink of the Screen*, 2012), A. S. Byatt, whose reviews had championed Pratchett's work, wrote of the 'quite extraordinary narrative pull of a great storyteller' and his development of character.[7] Such reviews began, to paraphrase the joke with which he responded in his publicity to these responses, to 'accuse' him of literature. More critical incomprehension was, though, evident as late as 2015 when the *Guardian*'s art correspondent reacted to Byatt's thoughtful and sympathetic review of Pratchett's last, posthumous, novel, *The Shepherd's Crown*, with a mean-spirited article by Jonathon Jones entitled 'Get real. Terry Pratchett is not a literary genius'. Jones's argument, not unreasonable in itself, that the recent deaths of Gabriel García Márquez and Gunter Grass had produced much less reaction among readers, would, as many readers (including fellow *Guardian* columnist Sam Jordison) responded, have had more weight if Jones had actually *read* some Pratchett, instead of 'flick[ing] through a book by him in a shop'.[8]

By that time a range of awards and honours had followed, including an OBE and a knighthood for services to literature. Pratchett had already been active in charity work. The popularity of his Librarian character led to support for the Orangutan Foundation, devoted to rescuing this endangered species. The wider attention given to him after his diagnosis with posterior cortical atrophy, a form of Alzheimer's disease, increased his public profile, as he met what he termed an 'embuggerance' with courage, humour and generosity, using his example to draw attention to the condition and raise money for the Alzheimer's Research Trust. He appeared in a two-part programme *Living with Alzheimer's* (BBC Television, 2009) and delivered the 2010 Richard Dimbleby lecture, devoted to his condition. Another television documentary, *Terry Pratchett: Choosing to Die* (2011), won numerous awards. After his death, the campaigner Jack Monroe adopted, with the support of Pratchett's estate, what she called the 'Vimes Index' (from Sam Vimes in *Men at Arms*, who reflects on how the rich can spend more money on better boots while poor people are constantly replacing cheaper but shoddier items) to show how higher commodity prices affect people with the least. This reflected an anger and concern for fairness which can increasingly be seen in his fiction.

In parallel, scholarship on Pratchett's work has progressed from showing that he is indeed 'guilty of literature' (the title of the first book of critical essays on him, published in 2000), to a significant body of work.[9] The 'official' Companions to Discworld published with Pratchett's involvement and blessing were met in 2001 by a slim 'Pocket Essential' handbook and in 2007 by a more substantial *Unofficial Companion*, both written/edited by Andrew M. Butler, while novelist Lawrence Watt-Evans added personal commentary in his 2008 survey *The Turtle Moves*.[10] More academic collections of essays include Jacob Held and James South's *Philosophy and Terry Pratchett* (2014), *Discworld and the Disciplines* (2014) edited by Anne Hiebert Alton et al., Nicholas Michaud's *Discworld and Philosophy: Reality Is Not What It Seems* (2016), Marion Rana's *Terry Pratchett's Narrative Worlds* (2018) and Justine Breton's *Power and Society in Terry Pratchett's Discworld: Building a Fantasy Civilization* (2025).[11] Of interest is the way his books, especially the Discworld series, engage with character and worldbuilding, and the problems which arise when books so closely focused upon English humour are translated into many languages. Important to many is the way his books illuminate issues of gender and identity. Pratchett's social anger is reflected in many critical studies, while Rebecca Ann Bach's monograph goes as far as suggesting, not altogether unseriously, that *Terry Pratchett Could Save the World* (2023).[12]

***

Terry Pratchett was born in Beaconsfield, Buckinghamshire on 28 April 1948, the only child of David Pratchett, a motor mechanic, and his wife, Eileen Florence, née Kearns, a secretary. His family encouraged his omnivorous range of interests, including amateur radio and astronomy. His mother paid for touch-typing lessons after his sale of 'The Hades Business' to *Science Fantasy* in 1963 enabled him to buy a typewriter.

While a trainee reporter on the *Bucks Free Press*, he wrote stories for the children's section. He also began a novel, *The Carpet People*, eventually published by a local firm, Colin Smythe Ltd, in 1971. Two science fiction books followed, *The Dark Side of the Sun* and *Strata*. *The Colour of Magic* and *The Light Fantastic* began the Discworld series: humorous fantasies set on a flat world (a notion

4

which had appeared in *Strata*) supported by four elephants on the back of a giant turtle 'swimming' through space. They introduced various settings and characters: Unseen University; Rincewind, the cowardly failed wizard; the Luggage, a sentient, legged trunk originally belonging to the tourist, Twoflower; Cohen the Barbarian, and Death. The parodic elements proved successful with fantasy readers. The Corgi paperback of *The Colour of Magic* displayed the front-cover blurb 'Jerome K. Jerome meets *Lord of the Rings* (with a touch of *Peter Pan*)'. While this now reads as a rather desperate attempt to 'place' the author, it is certainly true that Pratchett, is, like Jerome (the author of *Three Men in a Boat*, 1889), a sharply observant comic writer and a stylist whose work is immediately recognisable. In this, he stands with forebears such as W. C. Sellar and R. J. Yeatman's *1066 And All That* (1930), P. G. Wodehouse's Jeeves and Wooster stories (1915–1974) and Geoffrey Willans and Ronald Searle's Molesworth books (1953–1959).

In 1980, following periods at the *Western Daily Press* and the *Bath Evening Chronicle*, Pratchett became a publicity officer for the Central Electricity Generating Board. The success of the Discworld novels, following a co-publishing deal with a major hardback publisher, Victor Gollancz, allowed him to become a full-time writer in 1987. Former publisher Colin Smythe became his agent.

Less a continuing series than a set of interlinked sub-series upon the same stage, Discworld came to incorporate forty-one novels, short stories, maps, diaries/calendars, quiz books, four 'science of' books, authorised and unauthorised handbooks, guides and other reference works. Books originating in the Discworld universe came to appear as actual editions. *Where's My Cow?* and *The World of Poo* are based on books read by Sam Vimes to his son in the novels *Thud!* and *Snuff*. (*The World of Poo*, in which "Miss Felicity Beadle" opens up the world of scatology to young readers, is a particularly entertaining example of the way Pratchett exploited his research.) There are also stage adaptations by Stephen Briggs, role-playing games, film/video, television and radio adaptations, music albums, audiobooks, comic books, merchandise figurines, commemorative stamps and varieties of beer.

Unrelated humour (*The Unadulterated Cat*) and children's

books (The Bromeliad trilogy and the Johnny Maxwell series) proved popular. The third Johnny Maxwell novel, *Johnny and the Bomb*, won the 1996 Smarties Prize Silver Award. *The Amazing Maurice and His Educated Rodents*, a Discworld novel written separately from the main sequence as a children's novel, won the Chartered Institute of Library and Information Professionals Youth Librarian Group's Carnegie Award for best children's book of the year. *Good Omens*, a collaboration with Neil Gaiman, eventually gained massive posthumous success as a Gaiman-scripted TV adaptation on Amazon Prime (2019), followed by a second series in 2021 bringing the characters into new territory. Pratchett, however, continued with Discworld, which progressed from affectionate satire of post-Tolkien fantasy to become a remarkable deconstruction of absurdity in all walks of life, with a recurring cast of witches, wizards, Watchmen (of numerous species), and metaphoric personifications such as the skeletal Death – complete with scythe and pale horse – who speaks in block capitals and is puzzled by the foibles of humanity.

Unlike most series fantasy, Discworld never stagnated. Put simply – it was something he admitted in interviews – Pratchett improved as a writer. By the 1990s, humour had moved well beyond simple parody. Threats to the stability of the Discworld such as the 'beings from the Dungeon Dimensions' – a nod to the monstrosities of horror writer H. P. Lovecraft or caricatures like Trymon in *The Light Fantastic*, whose obsession with organisation undermines the bumbling anarchy of Unseen University – were replaced in later novels such as *Hogfather* and *Thief of Time* by the 'Auditors of Reality' whose aim is to 'rationalise' the universe by eliminating individuality and personality. His sometimes-deceptive playfulness frequently brought readers suddenly to the realisation that comic figures such as the trainee witch Magrat Garlick, or Sam Vimes, the stereotype drunken cop, have become *characters*. Non-Discworld novels allowed Pratchett to flex his imagination and exploit his prodigious capacity for research. *Nation* explored colonial contact between Pacific Islanders and the British in an alternative nineteenth century. *Dodger* included as characters the eponymous artful sewer-scavenger who becomes involved in an international conspiracy, Charles Dickens and Henry Mayhew (whose observations of the life of the London poor were mined in Pratchett's research for the book). Towards the end of his life, Pratchett returned to science fiction, with a series of books written in collaboration with Stephen Baxter, himself an important British sf writer.

Pratchett's books had been translated into thirty-eight languages by the time of his death, and he several times topped British bestseller lists. He received numerous awards in the fields of fantasy and science fiction. *Pyramids* won the 1989 British Science Fiction Association award. *Going Postal* was nominated for the 2005 World Science Fiction Convention's Hugo Award for best novel. *The Wee Free Men, A Hat Full of Sky, Wintersmith* and *The Shepherd's Crown* were named as best Young Adult books of the year by the influential *Locus* magazine, which also awarded *Making Money* Best Fantasy Novel. He was fantasy and science fiction author of the year in the 1994 British Book Awards. As with his critical reception, such recognition expanded into the wider literary sphere. In 2010, the same year he received the World Fantasy Award for life achievement, he tied with Martin Amis as winner of the National Book Awards Outstanding Achievement award.

In 1998 he was made an OBE for services to literature. Various honorary degrees followed after an honorary DLitt from the University of Warwick in 1999. He was appointed adjunct professor at Trinity College, Dublin, in 2009. Knighted in 2009, he enlisted a local blacksmith to help him make the sword which every knight (especially a knight who was a fantasy writer) should have. 'For someone whose life was devoted to working with the intangible, the creation of something so emphatically solid – and by properly ancient means – brought immense joy'.[13] At his funeral, his daughter Rhianna carried this sword, made from iron ore from his own land.

2

The Early Works

BEFORE DISCWORLD

'The Hades Business', expanded from a story originally published in his school magazine, suggested 'great promise for the future' according to the editor of *Science Fantasy*, John Carnell.[1] By the time of his second appearance in a science fiction magazine ('Night Dweller', *New Worlds*, 1965), Pratchett was a trainee reporter writing children's stories as 'Uncle Jim' for the *Bucks Free Press*. These early stories (reprinted much later in book form) became a store of ideas for re-use in later novels. The town of Blackbury, for instance, reappears in the Johnny Maxwell books, and the Store-dwelling 'nomes' of Truckers can be traced back to the 1973 *Bucks Free Press* story 'Rincemangle, the Gnome of Even Moor', whose protagonist also foreshadows Rincewind of *The Colour of Magic* (*ABOTS* 48–60). These stories gave him experience in the discipline of writing tightly formatted entertainment at speed for a defined readership. These young readers of the children's page formed an inexperienced audience who needed broad-brush, immediate storytelling; Pratchett's attendance at science fiction conventions though had also exposed him to potential readers who could be expected to understand his topical allusions and be aware of conscious and unconscious borrowings from a wide range of literature. The initial result was *The Carpet People* – an at-times uneasy fusion of the two audiences drawing upon some of his Uncle Jim stories mixed with his reading of Tolkien, still recent enough for him to uncritically echo. He was to revise the 1992 reprint extensively, remarking that it was written at a time when he thought that fantasy was about battles and kings, but *rewritten* now believing that 'the real concerns of fantasy ought to be about not having battles, and doing without kings' (*CP2* 10).

The 'Carpet People' are the Munrungs and other inhabitants of the Carpet, threatened by the orcish Mouls and the threat of Fray, aided by Bane/Baneus Catrix, clearly influenced by Tolkien's Aragorn/Strider. Some of the writing of the novel was shared with his fellow convention-goer and friend Edward James, who later became a professor of medieval history and one of Britain's leading experts on sf and fantasy. Writing about it in 2004, James called it 'a genuinely original piece of fantasy, which took the tropes of genre fantasy seriously [...] and had the excitement of his young audience constantly in mind', perhaps 'disembowelled' in the reprint by the concern the forty-three year-old successful novelist had to tackle the inexperience and naivety of his teenage self.[2] While the story remains entertaining, one gets the impression (amusing in itself) of the older Pratchett impatiently trying to write the novel the younger Pratchett *ought* to have written. Pseudo-Tolkien formal speech is rewritten more colloquially. Pismire the Gandalfian 'magician' becomes 'the shaman, a kind of odd-job priest', and another mysterious Wight magician, Culain, becomes Culaina, a woman who 'knows all possibilities' foreshadowing Esk in the much later *I Shall Wear Midnight* and *The Shepherd's Crown* (*CP2* 11, 19, 154–161). Issued in an edition of 3,000 copies, *The Carpet People* was still in print ten years later, but it had cemented the relationship with Colin Smythe Ltd which resulted in two 'adult' science fiction novels, *The Dark Side of the Sun* and *Strata*.

THE SEEDS OF DISCWORLD

Pratchett's first novel for adults is, John Clute suggests, something of a 'gambol'[3] – or even a *gamble* in the way he, like many early-career writers, seems to be throwing as many ideas as he can into the mix in case he never gets a chance to use them again. *The Dark Side of the Sun* is an inventive – perhaps over-inventive – snapshot of a baroque sf future, throwing information at us using the familiar device of a 'Galactic Chronicle' (in the manner of Isaac Asimov's 'Encyclopedia Galactica' in the Foundation series) to check, off for instance, 'races classed as Human' in a complex universe. The novel's 'p-math' (which predicts *that* the hero will be killed, though not *how*) clearly echoes Asimov's fictional science of 'psycho-history' through which future social trends can be predicted. The ingenious roster of aliens, including a vanished super-race, the Jokers, owes much to those of another American sf writer, Larry Niven, author of the popular novel *Ringworld* (1970), which, like *Strata*, also featured a 'constructed' world. Sidebar wit (when Dom is challenged 'Enemy or Friend of Earth' (*DSOTS* 17), the right answer is of course 'FOE') evokes the work of Robert Sheckley, whose comic vein of sf, such as the novel *Dimension of Miracles* (1968) may have also influenced Douglas Adams's *The Hitchhiker's Guide to the Galaxy*. The line from a song, 'I must scream yet I have no mouth' (*DSOTS* 370) knowingly nods to readers remembering Harlan Ellison's 'I Have no Mouth and I Must Scream' published in the magazine *IF* (March 1967). Already, Pratchett is picking up common-stock sf ideas and starting to tinker with them.

If Discworld is a construction, its building-blocks rapidly developing from generic trappings borrowed from others into something we can point to and say 'Pratchettian', the pieces of *DSOTS* have yet to coalesce from what we may call the soup of story (see chapter 5). They nevertheless contain intriguing signals of what is to come. The implication of p-math and the series of deaths inflicted upon Dom Sabalos in his search for the Jokers' world suggests that 'in an infinite Totality all universes will happen' (*DSOTS* 23) – an idea foreshadowing the Long Earth series (Pratchett's collaboration with Stephen Baxter) and the 'trousers of time' image in Discworld and the Johnny Maxwell series. There are some leaden jokes. The playful allusiveness does not always work, most notably when we discover that the Jokers' world 'lies at the dark side of the sun'. (*DSOTS* 68) – an expression too much like Asimov's Star's End as the location of his Second Foundation to carry the weight the plot demands. There are, however, genuinely interesting and imaginative inventions, which turn out, with the benefit of hindsight, to be seeds of Discworld: 'Hogswatchnight', 'Soul Cake Friday', and 'the Eve of Small Gods'. The reflection that 'a student of probability soon realizes that by its nature the billion-to-one chance crops up nine times out of ten' (*DSOTS* 46) is the first appearance of a favourite Discworld joke.

The next novel, *Strata*, is in part a development of '[o]n some worlds we had to build an entirely new crust, down to the fossils' (*DSOTS* 156). In it, we can see this idea – a parody of a common trope of artificially 'built' worlds – becoming something that can be used as a setting. It begins as another gambol – or gamble – fusing humour with invention more confidently, with Kin Arad, in charge of a planet-building team, scolding a pair of subordinates who have done what everyone – including her – has done: inserted an anomaly in the strata. (In this case, a plesiosaur holding a placard worded 'End nuclear testing now'.) An intruder appears in her office: someone with the secret of invisibility. He has information about other 'impossible' technologies, ascribed to the 'Great Spindle Kings', now-extinct planet-builders who lived 400 million years ago.

The influence of Larry Niven is once again strong: the ferocious-looking bear-like 'shand' who is one of Arad's companions in her quest to uncover the history of her universe is very much indebted to the 'kzin' in *Ringworld* and elsewhere. This is another device that paradoxically identifiably echoes the work of others while vividly announcing an original and fertile imagination. It is, however, the discovery of a flat world and Arad's adventures upon it which both confirms Pratchett's structuring of the novel as both parody of/homage to Niven's acclaimed *Ringworld* and the way his imagination was already playing with the idea. Although this is a science fiction novel, with a flat Earth constructed by alien planetary engineers, the idea of a flat world resting upon the backs of four elephants standing upon a space-swimming turtle appears in conversation as the team approaches this proto-Discworld (*St* 58). Fantasy elements appearing as re-creations or echoes of our own history include Vikings, dragons, and a realm whose 'Arabian Nights' clichés offer jokes whose bathos could easily find a place in Discworld. A demon speaks in capital letters, like Death in the Discworld series. One joke, in which Kin Arad, attempting to lie convincingly, is advised to 'sue your face for slander', reappears almost verbatim in the first Discworld book, while the name of a bar, the Broken Drum, also carries over (*St* 177, 35).

Although *Strata* seems to suffer, in the end, from conflicting aims as parody or straightforward serious 'homage', it does introduce some of the ethical and philosophical arguments which find a place in Pratchett's later work. A conversation between Silver and another alien companion, Marco, is reminiscent of how Pratchett portrays cultural conflicts in multi-species Discworld: 'We have been around humans too long, you and I [...] we learn to speak monkey languages that monkey tongues can handle, and we get along in their world' (*St* 170). Pratchett's later engagement with the way in which stories we tell about the world *become* the world – the 'thing that dreams while the rest of us is asleep' that builds the universe (*St* 190) – is rather clumsily expressed in the language of science fiction rather than the more playful metaphorical mode of fantasy. But it is there, and although *Dark Side* and *Strata* were published and sold in relatively small quantities – the 1982 New English Library paperback edition of 5,000 copies was remaindered in 1985[4] – they were favourably reviewed.

For his fourth novel for Colin Smythe, Pratchett decided that he would return to fantasy to exploit his skills as a comic writer and 'do for fantasy fiction what *Blazing Saddles* had done for the western'.[5] In doing so, he would return to the idea which, he felt, had by no means been exhausted in *Strata*.

DISCWORLD TAKES SHAPE

In November 1983, Colin Smythe Ltd issued a 500-copy edition of *The Colour of Magic*, less a novel than four linked short stories set on a Discworld resting upon the shoulders of four elephants – Berilia, Tubul, Great T'Phon and Jerakeen – standing on the back of a gigantic star-turtle, Great A'Tuin. Its popularity among readers open to parody of the numerous blockbuster fantasies which had exploited the success of *The Lord of the Rings* resulted in a sequel, *The Light Fantastic*, continuing the adventures of the incompetent wizard Rincewind and the naïve Twoflower. If the various heroes created by novelist Michael Moorcock (editor of *New Worlds* in which Pratchett's second professional sf story appeared) form the Eternal Champion, Rincewind is the Eternal Coward (*LC* 40) whose value to the forces manipulating him is that he is a born survivor: his response to anything is to flee. Twoflower is the Eternal Tourist whose spectacles are thoroughly rose-coloured. Rincewind is, in fact, nothing more than a pawn in a game played by two of the Discworld's gods. Twoflower is a visitor from an enormously powerful empire initially encoded with generic Oriental stereotypes, although Péter Hajdu, analysing the later novel *Interesting Times* in which Rincewind and Twoflower are reunited, argues that Twoflower initially 'represented the stereotypes of an American rather than a Chinese tourist'.[6] Like many tourists, he sees the superficially exotic. The danger and squalor of the city of Ankh-Morpork and the brigand-haunted Broken Drum are simply picturesque and quaint. He speaks the local language in phrase-book quotations and carries around with him an imp-powered 'iconograph' and a homicidally dangerous trunk, the Luggage.

The Colour of Magic and *The Light Fantastic* can be seen as two parts of a single novel. They are treated as such in the 2008 two-part television adaptation *The Colour of Magic*, which incorporates the overall story – there is both the imminent destruction of the world to prevent and Great A'Tuin's goal to work out – in a way much less episodic than Pratchett's originals, where we are left, in the first volume, with an almost literal cliffhanger. Reading the duology in the context of its many successors, Pratchett is still feeling his way. The influence of his teenage reading is still strong, particularly that of fantasy writer Fritz Leiber, whose 'massive-walled and mazy-alleyed metropolis of Lankhmar, thick with thieves and shaven priests, lean-framed magicians and fat-bellied merchants'[7] seems to be revisited in '[t]he twin city of proud Ankh and pestilent Morpork, of which all the other cities of time and space are, as it were, mere reflections' (*COM* 15). Two sword-and-sorcery barbarians, Bravd and the Weasel, appear: clear reflections of Leiber's Fafhrd and Gray Mouser. The satire of sword-and-sorcery, though, is aimed at the work of another writer. Robert E. Howard's Conan the Barbarian may 'tread the jeweled thrones of the Earth under his sandaled feet',[8] but the 'legend in his own lifetime' Rincewind meets is in his eighties and still waiting for the royalties from the songs the bards composed about him. While the greatest thing in life for a barbarian hero in his prime may be 'the sight of your enemy slain, the humiliation of his tribe and the lamentation of his women', for the elderly *Cohen*, it is now 'good dentishtry and shoft lavatory paper' (*LF* 48).

Cohen, who reappears in *Interesting Times* and *The Last Hero*, is one of several characters (and/or anthropomorphic personifications) appearing in the first two novels. Most important, in terms of the way they are repeated and developed in succeeding novels, are the Librarian, Death and the Patrician, Vetinari. The Librarian first appears in an almost throwaway episode when a blast of magic in *The Light Fantastic* turns him into an orangutan, but Pratchett's passion for libraries as a home for autodidacts made it almost inevitable that the relationship between knowledge and books would develop into a rich vein of comedy. Death similarly appears as a joke in *The Colour of Magic*, drawing upon the folk-tale about the merchant's servant who, encountering Death in the market, flees to another town – where Death had an appointment with him. The incongruity of a skeletal supernatural figure puzzled by humanity soon fashions a useful central character. The Patrician, the 'tyrant' ruling Ankh-Morpork, is unnamed in *The Colour of Magic* and, like Twoflower, is described differently from his initial appearance in later books, but he is recognisably the Machiavellian Vetinari who manipulates others for the good of the State. Contradictions are resolved by Pratchett's later response to fans: 'How about: maybe he was Vetinari, but written by a more stupid writer?'.[9]

Less important in the overall picture of Discworld as it develops, but a generically important prop for story-dynamics, are the creatures from the Dungeon Dimensions, hinted at in *Colour of Magic* but expanded in *Light Fantastic*, *Equal Rites*, *Sourcery*, *Eric* and others. They are among Pratchett's nods to H. P. Lovecraft, whose monstrous beings (Cthulhu, Nyarlathotep, Azathoth, Yog-Sothoth) and nihilistic emphasis on the insignificance of humanity chilled his audience in *Weird Tales* and elsewhere in the 1920s and 1930s and contributed to his popularity among horror-fiction readers in the 1960s. However, as genre-familiar emblems of monstrosity and unsettling chaos, they are almost immediately undercut by one of Pratchett's characteristic footnotes. Our universe is, for them 'the psychic equivalent of handy for the buses and closer to the shops' (*LF* 14). Though this strand immediately gets darker in *Equal Rites* and *Sourcery*, the quip itself is a recognition that for committed fans, their originals in Lovecraft's 'Cthulhu Mythos', become not so much sources of terror as expected, even cuddly, stereotypes. (Similarly, Pratchett's jokes about one of Lovecraft's characteristic words, 'eldritch', shares the way it became a humorous catchphrase among fans.) Pratchett was to turn to humanity for his more unsettling antagonists and villains, increasingly foregrounding the idea of people objectifying other people being what worried him rather than cloaking revulsion of the monstrous in human nature by inventing fictional 'things'. Trymon, the ambitious wizard in *The Light Fantastic*, is the first of Pratchett's bureaucratic villains, a man who can use management-speak jargon and mean it. A strand starting with Trymon's obsession with order and control becomes more important throughout the sequence, with Lupine Wonse in *Guards! Guards!*, Vorbis in *Small Gods* and Reacher Gilt of *Going Postal*, and of course the Auditors of Reality from *Reaper Man* to *Thief of Time* attempting to rearrange and subdue the messiness of everyday 'social' humanity.

Light Fantastic is an effective mixture of Conanesque sword-and-sorcery parody and topical jokes, such as the send-up of the then-recent craze for interpreting prehistoric stone circles as astronomical 'computers'. It even develops a climax in which Rincewind becomes something of an unlikely, if still two-dimensional, hero, triumphing over his cowardly nature. It is, however, with the third Discworld novel *Equal Rites* that Pratchett moves decisively beyond genre-parody.

Equal Rites, for the first time, delivers a solid plot, and introduces Discworld's witches. It centres upon Esk, the eighth-born child of an eighth son: that is, she would qualify to be a wizard if she had been a son rather than a daughter. The wizard Drum Billet passes his staff on to her when he dies, and her embryonic magical powers are noticed by the local witch Granny Weatherwax, who tries to get her enrolled in Unseen University which (like many Oxbridge colleges during the twentieth century) is unable to accept women until 'we get the plumbing sorted out' (*ER* 198). Granny is not quite the fleshed-out favourite of later novels. At one point she is described as clapping a 'warty hand' on someone's shoulder (*ER* 14); the later Granny does not have warts. At the end of the novel there is a hint of a romance with Archchancellor Cutangle of Unseen University. However, her threat to Esk's staff certainly foreshadows the angry moralist which becomes part of her character: 'First it'll be the spokeshave. And then the sandpaper and auger [...]' (*ER* 186). There is also her resistance to the chauvinist wizards and her insistence that most of witchcraft is not magic, but 'headology' (*ER* 43–44). Granny, along with Death and the Librarian, is among the earliest examples of Pratchett's increasingly successful technique of characters weaving in and out of multiple storylines. Some, such as Mrs Whitlow, the Unseen University Housekeeper, who reappears in *Interesting Times* to stir interesting emotions in the celibate wizards, remain minor characters. Others are recast; there is something of Hilta Goatfinder in the far more vivid Nanny Ogg, and the buzzing Lovecraftian 'Dungeon Dimensions' creatures become more abstract manipulative forces that, in *Moving Pictures*, intrude into the stability of Discworld.

Early episodes involving Esk as a child establish aspects of Discworld's 'magic' which continue to be developed for metaphorical effect. At one point, young Esk 'Borrows' (enters the mind of another being) and is nearly lost. It is, however, this ability which allows her, when her wizarding abilities are improved, to Borrow the mind of the University itself and open the door into the Dungeon Dimensions to rescue young Simon, whose innate magical abilities have astounded the wizards. Simon's theoretical approach opens a fantasy version of the more science-fictional 'infinite Totality' of *Dark Side of the Sun*, allowing Pratchett to develop new ideas and 'correct' inconsistencies because this can be allowed by the framework of the fictions. *Equal Rites* ends with Esk and Simon developing 'a whole new type of magic that no one could exactly understand' (*ER* 205), but we hear no more of Esk until *I Shall Wear Midnight* and *The Shepherd's Crown*, and only hints of Simon in the former.

Equal Rites reached a wider audience with its co-publishing deal with Gollancz and its radio serialisation, but already some of its core audience were wondering what Pratchett could do next. Barbara Davis, reviewing the novel in the British Science Fiction Association's *Vector* asked 'how many more Discworld books will there be? Could it be time for something completely different?'.[10] It is with the next few novels that Discworld is consolidated. It solidifies as an invented fantasy realm which expresses fantasy writers' and -readers' love of invention: the nineteenth-century fantasy writer George MacDonald's delight 'in calling up new forms which is the nearest, perhaps, [a writer] can come to creation' or what Tolkien in his essay 'On Fairy-stories' calls 'sub-creation'.[11] It moves from echoing the kind of fantasy-otherworld exemplified by Tolkien's Middle-earth or Leiber's Nehwon to become a wonderfully vivid case study of what Tolkien called, in his essay, 'the Cauldron of Story' (which will be discussed in chapter 5). It also, metafictionally, delights in parodying the 'delight' of MacDonald (and Tolkien's readers) in the way that another fantasy writer, Diana Wynne Jones, highlighted genre clichés in her *Tough Guide to Fantasyland* (1996).[12] In doing so, Pratchett instils in his humour, as Mendlesohn and James note, a 'sense of purpose', increasingly asking 'some of the awkward questions' avoided by many fantasy writers.[13] This process begins with the feminist message of *Equal Rites*, a message perhaps undermined by the ambiguous ending but which returns much more strongly with *Mort*.

This is the first Discworld novel to focus upon one of the ongoing characters and examine them. In this case, it is Death. 'Mort' means, of course, 'death', but it is also short for Mortimer, the youth who, unfit for steady employment elsewhere, is hired as Death's apprentice. Doing his best to carry out his Master's duties with minimal instruction, Mort manages to disrupt history by saving the Princess Keli, whom he is sent to 'reap'. We follow Mort's maturing and Death's contradictions through a novel in which humour is counterpointed with moral observations. Pratchett's version of the Grim Reaper has a fondness for cats and curry and an endearing inability to understand people. There are jokes about how Mort, as an apprentice, may 'take over the business' and marry Death's adopted daughter Ysabel. However, part of the humour – and the moral undercurrent of the story – depends upon the deconstruction of a running joke about there being 'no justice'. Death agrees. THERE'S JUST ME (*M* 41). Furthermore, Death cannot allow concepts like Fairness and Compassion to muddle his duty. When Mort tries to warn a king that he is about to be murdered, he is admonished and warned that if he feels compassion it should manifest in what is appropriate to his trade: a sharp edge to his scythe. The 'no justice' joke is turned around to become THERE'S JUST YOU, as Death reminds Mort of duty and personal responsibility, and again when Death himself is asked to 'own' his own meddling in the fates of others.

Saving Keli's life results in a historical paradox. For the wider course of Discworld history, she was 'meant' to have been killed by her wicked uncle, who would then unite neighbouring kingdoms. There are now two separate realities entangling as History tries to revert to its original shape. The paradox resolves with both Mort and Death recognising their own personal responsibilities. Death must not interest himself in human affairs any longer (an abdication soon relinquished in *Reaper Man* and *Hogfather*) and Mort must make sure that history takes place.

The next novel, *Sourcery*, returns to Ankh-Morpork and Unseen University. There is a new Archchancellor-designate, Virrid Wayzygoose, but no memory of *Equal Rites*'s Cutangle, who may have died, or may even not have existed in this reality. Similarly, there is no mention of Esk and Simon. It is hard not to read *Sourcery* as a major underlining and rounding-off of a 'first draft' of Discworld. The concept of 'sourcery' – the wild, original magic of ancient times – was first mentioned as an aside in *Equal Rites* in a comment about Simon. Here it is applied to Coin, eighth son of a wizard, who cheats Death by incorporating his soul into his staff. Under the staff's influence, Coin makes his way to Unseen University, where he proclaims himself Archchancellor and increases the power of the University and the Wizards, eventually reimagining Anhk-Morpork itself. The scene is set for a violent magical confrontation between Coin and the traditional Archchancellors' Hat, taken by Rincewind to the city of Al Khali, whose ruler, the Seriph, is the butt of a series of Arabian Nights jokes from spoof Omar Khayyam poetry to the erotic stimulus of storytelling. A complicated series of confrontations results. Discworld is restored to its former state. Coin retreats from the world. Rincewind's fate sets him up for forthcoming books.

If *Mort* was an attempt to use the Discworld as a stage-setting to explore some awkward questions about responsibility, *Sourcery* was perhaps a step backwards in its introduction of parodic characters such as Creosote the Seriph, Nijel the Destroyer, the trainee 'barbarian hero' who learns his trade from a handbook, and Conina, daughter of Cohen the Barbarian who has inherited her father's skills but would much rather be a hairdresser. It was, however, well received by readers and reviewers, with Tom Hutchinson in the *Times* noting that 'he puts in the intellectual boot' and that behind the humour 'is a memorable account of how we adapt power before it adapts us'.[14]

Was the rebuilding of reality at the end of *Sourcery* a shift into a version where Esk and Simon's new type of magic, and a 'progressive' touch to the hidebound University was not developed? Penny Hill suggests the sweeping-away of the history of *Equal Rites* implies that it 'is set in a parallel universe to that of the subsequent novels'.[15] Perhaps what we are seeing is less deliberate structuring and more a simple wiping of the board to allow the incorporation of changes as better ideas come forward. Such wiping-rewriting is made possible by the reality-tinkering conclusions at the end of the early Discworld novels, but while the 'rebooting' of such major franchises as *Star Trek* and *Star Wars* and the constant tinkering with 'canon' in long-running programmes like *Doctor Who* allows the life of the franchise to be extended, there is only so far such reality-changing can take us. The novels up to *Sourcery* show us a writer beginning to understand what fertile ground is coming under his command, and getting away with changing aspects of Discworld that have little creative potential remaining in them. Rincewind is safely 'parked' to allow other characters to develop, while *Mort*'s experiment with expanding what is at first a secondary character and putting human nature at centre-stage offered a model to follow. Wholesale re-mapping of the sequence was eventually jettisoned in favour of a more nuanced playfulness with the introduction of the History Monks of *Small Gods*, *Thief of Time* and *Night Watch*, whose task it is to preserve history.

Sourcery began with an author's note: 'This book does not contain a map. Please feel free to draw your own' (*So* tp: verso). From the following novel, *Wyrd Sisters*, Discworld began to take a much deeper moral and imaginative shape. Between 1993 and 1999, Stephen Player, in collaboration with Pratchett, produced four maps, of Ankh-Morpork, Discworld, Lancre and Death's Domain. Increasingly charted, the sequence developed its own momentum in a rich mixture of related series, sub-series, and location and character development.

3

Mapping Discworld

Most Discworld books can be read as stand-alones. Pratchett's centring of theme or subject (*Macbeth* in *Wyrd Sisters*, opera in *Maskerade*, the Hollywood film industry in *Moving Pictures*, football in *Unseen Academicals*) focuses the jokes. But recurrence and repetition of setting and characters allow us to construct series, even sub-series. *Men at Arms* and *Making Money* are direct sequels (to *Guards! Guards!* and *Going Postal*). More generally, we see the Unseen University wizards, once power-hungry Sourcerers, now ivory-tower academics with a fondness for large meals, contrasted with the rural witches, equally anarchic and competitive but more focused upon ideas of community and duty. Occasionally, as in *Equal Rites* and *Lords and Ladies*, this conflict is direct.

With the fifth Discworld novel, *Wyrd Sisters*, Pratchett settled down to exploring Discworld's imaginary geography, expanding caricature into character and beginning the Witches series. This eventually covered *Witches Abroad*, *Lords and Ladies*, *Maskerade* and *Carpe Jugulum*, plus the associated Tiffany Aching series for young adults: *The Wee Free Men*, *A Hat Full of Sky*, *Wintersmith* and *I Shall Wear Midnight*. *The Shepherd's Crown*, Pratchett's final novel, in which Granny Weatherwax dies and Tiffany succeeds her as 'the most highly-regarded of the leaders [witches] didn't have' (*WS* 7), may or may not have been intended to round-off the series, but it was by no means intended to be the final Discworld novel.

Beginning with a desolate moor and an 'eldritch voice' shrieking the famous opening from *Macbeth*'s 'three witches' scene, Pratchett also shifted reader expectations of fantasy to collective memory of other 'cultural artefacts'. *Macbeth* has three witches, and the famous question 'Is this a dagger?'. It has a weak lord pulled into regicide by an ambitious wife, and a rightful heir who escapes. So, therefore, does *Wyrd Sisters*, although the obligatory Ghost is closer to that in *Hamlet*, as is the use of plays and players to present a loaded version of events. *Macbeth* may not feature a Fool, but the capering Fool in Duke Felmet's court is, like Shakespeare's, a voice which may speak to power, but only in constrained and coded forms. Even his repertoire of quips and riddles, 'prithee' and 'marry' is prescribed, standardised and archaic. Although he loathes what the Duke and Duchess are doing, his role, as with his counterpart in *King Lear*, condemns him to unconditional loyalty. The 'dagger' joke becomes oddly poignant: not a 'dagger of the mind' but a grubby handkerchief offered by the Fool to his weeping master who, he suddenly understands, is completely insane. It is typical of Pratchett: once jokes are laughed at, they often segue into moments of insight, and *Wyrd Sisters* is a skilfully plotted novel in which the title foreshadows further developments.

WYRD TALES

'Wyrd' is significant. Folklorist Jacqueline Simpson notes the relationship of 'Wyrd' (rather than 'weird') to Fate or Destiny, and the three 'Fates' (Clotho, Lathesis and Atropos) in Greek mythology or the Norse Norns, Urðr, Verðandi and Skuld.[1] The playwright Hwel, hired to write a play justifying King Verence's murder by his brother Felmet, choses *three* witches who 'could be meddling in the destinies of mankind' (*WS* 179). Meanwhile, Granny Weatherwax plans to enable Tomjon, hidden among Hwel's players, to return and claim his destiny as heir. The three Lancre witches – Esme 'Granny' Weatherwax, Gytha 'Nanny' Ogg and Magrat Garlick – have, following another set of folklorish customs, become 'fairy godmothers' and granted Tomjon gifts – friendship, a good memory, and the ability to be 'whoever he thinks he is' – that will not only affect his destiny but also undermines the simple narrative they had in mind. The usurper Felmet is concerned to confirm his own destiny by commissioning the 'propaganda' play; after all, words can change the world and *history* is what people are *told*. Whether

'Fate', 'Destiny' or simply, as will be discussed later, 'Story', personal narratives are increasingly foregrounded. The Fool is allowed to step out of his allotted role because his identity is not what was assumed. The repeated joke about Verence's *droit de seigneur*, which goes completely over Magrat's head, is the clue.

The Wyrd Sisters, Granny (familiar, in a slightly different form, from *Equal Rites*), Nanny and Magrat are the 'Crone', 'Mother', 'Maiden' of popular Wiccan lore. Granny is moral and fierce. Her story, as Stacie Hanes notes 'is almost entirely about choice'.[2] She rejects a scripted life not only her own, but for others; in *Lords and Ladies* though she admits to the possibility that her youthful relationship with Mustrum Ridcully, who became Archchancellor of Unseen University, might in another possible phase-space have been happy. (This relationship was, apparently, never consummated: Granny, following medieval European tradition, remains 'qualified' to control a unicorn.) In *Witches Abroad*, her antagonist is her sister Lily, convinced that *she* is the 'good one' while constricting the people of Genua into roles formed by the story-logic of fairy tale. Granny is the moral centre of the series.

Nanny is bawdily comic. It is easy to see her in *Witches Abroad* discovering the delights of a 'banana dak'ry', asking waiters at a Genua high-society ball for ketchup, or flirting with the dwarf Casanunda, the Discworld's 'second greatest lover', as simple comic relief. In later novels, though, she is a pragmatic check upon the others, each struggling with their roles while Nanny herself happily seizes opportunities for pleasure. She admits, in the story 'The Sea and Little Fishes', to having become a witch to get boys, while Esme did so to get 'even' (*ABOTS* 266). In *Carpe Jugulum*, when Agnes suggests that her alter ego Perdita is that part of her which embodies transgressive fantasies, Nanny responds with '*I've* always been that part of me' (*CJ* 91). Nanny may have a soft spot for the Elf-King in *Lords and Ladies* who as 'Horned God' is a primal sexual being, but she is also a mother, desiring a world without threats to her children. As the capital-M 'Mother' in the tripartite scheme, she is the Matriarch who instructs her sons, terrorises her daughters-in-law, and dotes upon her appalling 'sweetie'-obsessed grandchild Pewsey. In her cameo appearance in *Thief of Time*, she plays another role associated with maternity: she is the archetypal midwife. Nanny is perhaps 'deep down, the most powerful of the witches' but she prevents people from finding this out.[3]

Magrat, at first a comically pathetic satire of New Age occultism, becomes more active and powerful throughout *Lords and Ladies* and *Carpe Jugulum*. Still resentful of her junior position in *Lords and Ladies*, she is unsure whether being Queen will mean anything more than holding court, doing tapestry and providing an heir. The threat to the Castle (and to her forthcoming marriage) from invading Elves turns her into a woman refusing her subordinate role. This growth continues throughout *Carpe Jugulum*, in which Magrat, now wife and mother, defends her realm against the intrusion of vampires. She appears briefly in *The Shepherd's Crown* where, now a mature woman, she is in a position to address Letitia, from a position of superiority, as 'My dear' (*SC* 269).

The Elves' intrusion spurs plot developments in a way typically skilful of Pratchett by now allowing early scenes to foreshadow a complex series of relationships and ideas resonating throughout the novel, and in some cases reappearing several novels down the line. One such is the challenge to Granny Weatherwax from Diamanda, leader of young would-be witches meeting at a stone circle marking the boundary between two worlds. This introduces Agnes/Perdita Nitt, brought forward in *Carpe Jugulum* and *Maskerade* to take over Magrat's role as maiden when marriage disqualifies her from the role.

TIFFANY ACHING

Technically part of the Witches sequence, the five Tiffany Aching volumes – the series 'I would most like to be remembered for'[4] – are somewhat aside from the main Discworld narrative. This is partly because they are (like *The Amazing Maurice and His Educated Rodents*) specifically written for children; partly because a sense of place (the chalk downs) runs all the way through them. The Weatherwax-Ogg-Garlick 'coven' appears, as mentors (along with a network of other witches) to Tiffany, who is nine in *The Wee Free Men* and progresses to her late teens in *The Shepherd's Crown*. The books are thus a story of a young girl growing up and embracing her position as a witch, a position which involves saving the world from supernatural threats but more importantly understanding that being a witch involves accepting responsibility for the powerless and voiceless. In the first novel, Tiffany discovers her abilities when she rescues her little brother and Roland, the son of the local Baron, from the Fairy Queen. In this, she has the sometimes-exasperating help of the anarchic Nac Mac Feegle, allegedly expelled from Fairyland for drunkenness and fighting.

In *A Hat Full of Sky*, Tiffany is eleven, an apprentice establishing herself among her fellow 'students' and defeating another intruding being, the identity-stealing 'hiver'. In *Wintersmith*, she is thirteen and training with Miss Treason, who takes her to witness the seasonal Dark Morris dance. Foolishly joining in, she attracts the attention of the personification of Winter, who seems to mistake her for his partner in the eternal dance of the seasons, the Summer Lady. Infatuated, the Wintersmith tries to make himself human and pursues Tiffany. In part a gentle and sensitive exploration of Tiffany's emotions and burgeoning sexuality, in part a romance of the cycle of the seasons, *Wintersmith*'s folk elements were emphasised by becoming a song-cycle by one of Pratchett's favourite bands, Steeleye Span. The Wintersmith's desire to 'make himself a man' and thus win Tiffany counterpoints Death's attraction to the paradox of humanity: the Wintersmith, recalling a once-heard musical piece, is 'astonished to find that a human being, nothing more really than a bag of dirty water on legs, could have such a wonderful understanding' (*WINT* 301). It was followed by *I Shall Wear Midnight*, in which fifteen-year-old Tiffany is reminded by questions from two younger girls how difficult relationships are for witches. Roland, once a potential partner, is now formal, even patronising, and apparently engaged. Furthermore, as Tiffany explains to her father, being a witch is dealing with things even well-meaning members of a community neglect to notice until too late. Such responsibility does not necessarily make a witch popular. Suspicions are made worse by the appearance on the scene of a spirit of hatred known as the Cunning Man, although Tiffany is helped once again by the Feegles, and by Roland's fiancée Letitia, a natural if untrained witch, and Eskarina Smith (Esk) from *Equal Rites*, who has become a mysterious time-travelling figure.

The Shepherd's Crown fuses the Tiffany and Witches series as Tiffany is eventually confirmed as natural heir to Granny Weatherwax. The Elf-Queen from *Lords and Ladies* (or a slightly different version) reappears. Posthumous publication meant that for many readers the death of a favourite character was combined with grief for the author's death, while its success as a novel is undermined by the difficulty of its composition as Pratchett's posterior cortical atrophy developed: 'Still the words came, but he was really having to cast around for them now'.[5] The published novel lacks a coda which Pratchett conceived during the writing but was unable to incorporate.[6]

SAM VIMES

After the Witches series, the most integrated series is perhaps the City Watch series, beginning with *Guards! Guards!* and continuing through *Men at Arms*, *Feet of Clay*, *Jingo*, *The Fifth Elephant*, *Night Watch*, *Thud!* and *Snuff*, with occasional cameo appearances elsewhere. Sam Vimes, the drunken commander of the disgraced and disgraceful Night Watch, is joined by Carrot, a human adopted by dwarfs. Carrott's idealism and devotion to duty upsets the culture of corrupt complacency into which the Watch has fallen. As Edward James aptly puts it, the series has both a hero (the viewpoint character Vimes, the Everyman character for whom 'justice means social justice and not just the capture of criminals') and a (capitalised) Hero, whose birthmark and oddly *un*magical sword, plus his strength and natural charisma, are clues that he is the rightful king of Ankh-Morpork.[7]

Carrot's seemingly naïve attention to the law is one thread in a complex tapestry, for Carrot can be seen as an essential third in a trinity consisting of himself, Vimes and the actual ruler of Ankh-Morpork, Vetinari. While the series begins in comic fashion with the washed-up Vimes as part of another trinity (fat and cowardly Sergeant Colon and inveterate scrounger Nobby) forming the dregs of the Night Watch, it becomes a debate about the rule of law and civilised society. 'Police' problems – conspiracy against Vetinari in *Guards! Guards!*, murder by means of an unknown weapon in *Men At Arms*, the poisoning of Vetinari in *Feet of Clay* and the theft of the Scone of Stone (upon which Dwarf Kings are crowned) in *The Fifth Elephant* – are counterpointed with deeper political issues as Vines progresses from Night Watch Commander to Duke of Ankh-Morpork. Vimes himself, initially cynical and beaten-down, is raised by his love for the aristocratic Sybil Ramkin, whose dragon-keeping saves the day in *Guards! Guards!*, and their son, whose need for a regular bedtime story provides a thread in *Thud!*, sympathetically highlighting Vimes's obsessive passions for justice and family life. Sybil herself progresses from being something of a figure of fun to a shrewd observer, especially when her husband's foibles and the prejudices of her schoolfellows are concerned. Pratchett's gift for allowing comedy to reveal complicated social issues can be shown in the way Nobby's sexuality becomes another running joke. This thread in *Jingo* is comic, slapstick, with references to music hall and the unsettling image of Nobby – who has to carry a certificate to prove his humanity – in drag. But even Nobby, trying to settle upon or even *find* his sexual nature, is not played entirely for unthinking laughs, as we find in later novels where his relationships with Verity Pushpram and the goblin Tears of the Mushroom are explored.

Vimes's sympathy for Ankh-Morpork's 'common people' is based upon a sense that the powerless, in essence 'no different from the rich and powerful except they've got no money or power' (*FOC* 269), must be defended from the powerful. Otherwise, he has no illusions about the virtues of the poor. Initially distrustful of the Dwarfs, Trolls, Golems, Werewolves, Vampires and other Discworlds 'races', he is equally distrustful of humanity. By *Night Watch*, a novel Pratchett's assistant Rob Wilkins called his 'masterpiece' and which has been published as a Penguin Modern Classic,[8] Vimes is aware of what he comes to call the Beast within him.

Night Watch highlights the mature Pratchett's literary techniques. It is, apparently, 'so little interested in in the motifs of fantasy literature that it's often easy to forget that this is Discworld'.[9] The novel's major fantasy trope is the transportation of Vimes into the past to become involved in the revolution which overthrew a previous Patrician. This, necessitating his assumption of the identity of his former mentor, John Keel, and his fatherly guiding of the sixteen-year-old recruit Sam Vimes, serves to highlight the novel as a dissection of identity. We are forced to ask who or what it is that Nobby and Reg and so on are commemorating at the start of the book – John Keel or 'John Keel'?[10] Pratchett's subtlety on this question of identity and role continues through to the next book, *Thud!*, when, in preparation for the inevitable Troll–Dwarf riots on the anniversary of their iconic battle at Koom Valley, Vimes and Fred Colon recall the barricades of over thirty years ago: 'It seems like only yesterday', recalls Vimes. To him, though not Fred, the events *were* much more recent (*Th* 162).

Here, we are far from the early novels' easy jokes and stereotypes. Vimes's conflict with his internal Beast returns in *Thud!* when he discovers the Summoning Dark, a quasi-demonic entity from Dwarf mythology expressed as a symbol which draws him to discover the truth about Koom Valley in a cavern beneath it. He refuses the luxury of giving way by evoking what he calls the Guarding Dark, who 'watches the Watchman', keeping the darkness inside from escaping. But Vimes is physically marked by the Summoning Dark. This linkage is returned to in *Snuff*, when Vimes's discovery that a young goblin woman has been murdered is hampered at first by his comic unfamiliarity with the mores of the countryside where he is holidaying with Sybil and Young Sam, and by the fact that goblins are not regarded as 'people' but, literally, 'vermin'. Once again Vimes resists the temptation to follow the psychopathic example of his adversary. It is tempting here to detect a sense of repetition after the success of *Night Watch*. The sequence shows Vimes growing as a character as he is exposed to new challenges and environments. *Snuff* certainly displays Pratchett's wit. Part of his depiction of what Vimes sees as the 'backward' nature of aristocratic country life includes the daughters of Sybil's friend Ariadne, all in need of husbands – Vimes even uses the 'truth universally acknowledged' allusion – one of whom is Jane, an uneasily perceptive young woman who has ambitions to write 'a novel about the complexities of personal relationships'(*Sn* 72). Her eventual title, which reworks that of Jane Austen's best-known novel to reflect Vimes's self-acknowledged underlying violence, is among Pratchett's finest throwaway wordplays. But hanging so much of the novel on yet another confrontation of Sam Vimes with his darker self seems like repeating familiar material. It is difficult to imagine how much further Pratchett could have taken Vimes.

RINCEWIND

We see much of Discworld outside Ankh-Morpork in the Witches sequence (which explores Genua in *Witches Abroad* and Überwald in *Carpe Jugulum*) and in the Watch sequence in *Jingo*, *The Fifth Elephant* and *Snuff*. The stand-alone *Pyramids* takes us to countries parodying Ancient Egypt and Classical Greece, and *Small Gods* is set in the lands between Klatch and Howondaland in the (or *a*) past of Discworld to confront scripture-based religion. Brutha, the last true believer, discovers his deity Om incarnated in the form of a small tortoise, and eventually transforms the bloody death-to-heretics Omnian faith into the well-meaning but constantly arguing religion exemplified by Constable Visit in the City Watch sequence and Mightily Oats in *Carpe Jugulum*. But it is in the sequence involving Rincewind that much of the mapping of Discworld is done.

After being trapped in the Dungeon Dimensions in *Sourcery*, Rincewind reappears in the illustrated novella *Eric*, summoned by a thirteen-year-old demonologist looking for a demon who will grant him his desires. Rincewind is something of a failure as Mephistopheles but, because of a sub-plot involving bureaucratic disputes in Hell, has power of a sort, if not *exactly* to the letter of Eric's demands. *Eric* successfully parodies *Faust* (strictly, it is entitled *Faust Eric*), and revisions Dante's *Inferno* in terms of modern management techniques. Episodes in Hell have some of the flavour of *Good Omens*, which Pratchett had been working on with Neil Gaiman. Rebellious demons eventually deal with their bureaucracy-loving overlord by promoting him out of harm's way – a tactic well-known in large organisations.

Recalled in *Interesting Times* (whose title refers to the apocryphal 'ancient Chinese curse' setting up the return to the Chinese-flavoured Agatean Empire), Rincewind becomes a pawn in Grand Vizier Hong's plan to undermine the Red Army which is conspiring against the Emperor. He is reunited with Twoflower, whose account of his time in Ankh-Morpork, *What I Did in My Holidays*, has become a revolutionary text, and Cohen the Barbarian, whose seven-man Silver Horde is there for one final theft. His return to Ankh-Morpork is mishandled by Ponder Stibbons's High Energy Magic Unit. Instead, he arrives in the mysterious continent known as XXXX (Fourecks), setting us up for *The Last Continent*.

Fourecks is Australia, a country Pratchett visited several times on book tours and holidays, and although the novel begins with a wittily accurate parody of that quintessentially *English* ceremony, the Tower of London's Ceremony of the Keys, the jokes play homage to Australian popular culture: films like *Mad Max* and *The Adventures of Priscilla, Queen of the Desert*, Australian slang, the national fondness for beer, and venomous insects. Rincewind finds himself, at one point, in a Gay Pride carnival, not quite understanding what is going on. His adventures overshadow the other half of the novel: the wizards' sojourn on a desert island with a god who has invented evolution. More balanced is *The Last Hero* where Rincewind volunteers (on the basis that he will inevitably *be* 'volunteered') to deal with Cohen the Barbarian's final adventure (storming Cori Celesti, the mountain of the gods at the Discworld Hub). Vetinari commissions Leonard of Quirm, the naïve inventor whose submarine was a feature of *Jingo*, to construct a spacecraft to allow Rincewind and Carrot to reach the Hub in advance of Cohen's Horde and ward off the disaster.

The Rincewind series suffers from the problem that he himself is a rather one-dimensional character who gets laughs by running away from danger. It is his 'cowardice' though – or reluctance to get killed – which makes him what Pratchett calls the eternal 'reasonable' character.[11] When told in *Interesting Times* that there are causes worth dying for, Rincewind emphatically denies this: 'you've only got one life but you can pick up another five causes on any street corner!' (*IT* 158) His cunning stands him in good stead as, in yet another million-to-one chance, he disseminates panic among the imperial army simply by denying rumours, which spread (increasing anxiety) even more. Much of the geography of Discworld is seen through Rincewind's adventures, but in *The Last Hero*, we observe it from outside. Within the humour is a still moment of sublimity as Carrot observes one of the elephants supporting the Discworld and struggles with his emotions, remarking wistfully as the continents below become visible that 'you can't see the boundaries between nations' (*TLH* 131).

DEATH

Although Death appears in most Discworld novels, a Death series can be formed from *Mort, Reaper Man, Soul Music, Hogfather* and *Thief of Time*. The last three are as much devoted to Susan Sto Helit, Death's granddaughter from Mort and Ysabel in *Mort*, and so, in *Guilty of Literature*, Stacie Hanes titles her essay 'Death and the Maiden' to focus on how Susan deals with being a semi-supernatural entity, drawn into carrying out Death's duty 'without having been created for it, without agreeing to do it, and without even knowing what it is'.[12] *Mort* begins a series exploring the nature of the anthropomorphic personifications of Discworld. The contradiction, as we find in the series of puns in *Mort* and succeeding novels, is that there is no justice, 'JUST ME'/'JUST US': personifications of the eternal verities and people who must make moral choices. *Mort* is weakened by everything being wound up because Death 'HAD A WORD WITH THE GODS' (*M* 219) – not quite 'with one bound, Jack was free', but approaching it. Nevertheless, it establishes a setting that becomes firmer with *Reaper Man*, whose layered structure illustrates its philosophy with poignant touches.

Death is dismissed by his superiors, the personality-less Auditors of Reality who return in *Hogfather* and *Thief of Time*. Distrusting living beings because emergent from 'Life' are such immaterial qualities as imagination, pity, hope and belief, they are also concerned that Death is developing a personality, beginning to care for humans. Death's absence causes problems, such as the inability of a wizard to actually *die* at the end of his life. The necessity of Death to get a job and form relationships counterpoints the wizard's needs to come to terms with being Undead (aided here by a self-help group led by Reg Shoe, a militant zombie). Sentenced to his own mortality, Death becomes farm labourer Bill Door, reaping a literal, instead of metaphorical, harvest. He saves the life of a child destined to die in a fire by 'loaning' her some of his life. When the New Death appears to take *him*, Death is loaned some of his employer Miss Flitworth's *own* life at a crucial moment when his plan to retaliate fails. Death's victory is a defeat for the Auditors, and an affirmation that while death itself is a necessary process it does not follow that it is evidence of a lack of compassion in the universe. There is still 'the care of the reaper man' (RM 231).

Soul Music introduces Susan, forced to take over Death's function when her grandfather abandons his duties. Death does what everyone does when they need to forget: he joins first the (Klatchian) Foreign Legion and then the squalid derelicts of Ankh-Morpork's lowest circles. The strand giving the novel its title, however, and around which the stories of Death and Susan revolve, is the trajectory which sends the harpist/guitarist Imp Y Celyn (Buddy) towards the destiny of all great rock stars. 'Music With Rocks In' transforms its listeners. It is transcendent, but, like the shopping-mall culture which infiltrates *Reaper Man* thanks to the Auditors' interference, it is parasitic. This paradox fuels jokes which are celebratory as well as satirical, depending upon their readers sharing and understanding the cultures that are mocked. Allusions to classic rock and roll songs are scattered throughout description and dialogue:

> 'Sometimes you do it for the money, but sometimes you do it for the show.'

> 'Hah! That'll be the day'. (*SM* 231).

Buddy and his band are destined for the fates which singers and bands loved by *Soul Music*'s readers meet – from Buddy Holly (whose name is referenced in 'Imp y Celyn') to Eddie Cochran, Otis Redding and Marc Bolan (one of whose nicknames was the 'bopping elf'): plane and car crashes are part of rock and roll mythology. Pratchett's increasing gift for counterpoint is highlighted by the hapless proto-punk band formed by Crash, Jimbo, Noddy and Scum, in the wake of The Band With Rocks In, who cannot even agree on a name (one of the truly great band names flies straight past them as they bicker) and who are so inept that even when they get their big chance to star (all attentive readers *know* this means they will win over the audience), they fall apart.

Susan's views on organising the world's fluffy thinkers are not far from many of Pratchett's villains, but unlike *Soul Music*'s bureaucrat-antagonist Mr Clete, she is idealistic. Finding it difficult to understand why Death did not intervene to save her parents, when her duty brings her to take the life of Imp y Celyn she is minded to refuse. Once again, the idea of destiny is the moral issue. Susan comes to realise that the sterile 'immortality' Death could have given Mort and Ysabel is different from 'more life'. Death understands that rules are sometimes guidelines. Occasionally the world *does* need changing.

Hogfather presents an older Susan as an impatient governess dealing with the belief of her charges in bogeymen under the bed by refusing to pander to their imaginations. She deals with actual monsters with an actual heavy poker. Having failed in *Soul Music*, the Auditors now attack human imagination at source by contracting with the Assassins Guild to eliminate one of the most potent icons of human creativity, the Hogfather, symbol of the Discworld's version of Christmas. Successful comic set pieces in the novel include the Good King Wenceslas story in which the peasant receives the King's charity whether he likes it or not, and, at greater length, Death's decision to substitute for the Hogfather in his absence. More confident in her role as part of the supernatural realm, Susan is also more determined to live her own life.

Thief of Time brings back the occasional rock and roll joke, the Auditors, and the History Monks, whose task it is to make sure history unfolds properly. Susan is now a teacher in a school run by a headmistress who has liberal ideas but is powerless against Susan's concern for discipline and hard work. The novel's plot is complex, but involves a master clockmaker hired by the Auditors to create a perfect clock. By accurately measuring the smallest possible amount of time, it will *freeze* time, destroying human unpredictability. This has happened before, explaining various discrepancies and paradoxes in history: we can be assured that what appeared to be contradictions or holes in previous novels are now due to the Monks' activities. The Auditors manifest as Lady Myria LeJean, who, to 'her' consternation, develops an identity. There is also another personification revealed in addition to the quartet of Death, War, Famine and Pestilence: a Fifth Horseman who, in the manner of Stuart Sutcliffe and the Beatles, 'left before they became famous' (*TOT* 218).

Nickianne Moody sees the Death series, as Rebecca Ann Bach sees *Feet of Clay*, as an examination of the idea of *work*.[13] It is the scythe with which Death does the work on Miss Flitworth's farm which defeats the New Death, rather than his own, symbolic, tool prepared by constant sharpening. When asked to destroy the scythe, the blacksmith Ned Simnel says 'This is old technology now. Redundant' (*RM* 151) reminding us that this is so for Death himself: 'The care which Death as an artisan brought to his craft is to be replaced by the inexorable quality of the production line or the combine harvester'.[14] Work is also central to the witches' duty, while in contrast wizards ostentatiously *avoid* work. Sam Vimes changes the Watch from a work-shy rabble to a disciplined unit. The golems in *Feet of Clay* 'do all the really mucky jobs' (*FOC* 122) but are 'abuse[d] [...] as if they were people'[15] and resented by those rendered 'surplus to requirements' by their ability to outperform skilled craftsmen (*FOC* 129). The idea of work is central to those books describing industrial and social changes in Ankh-Morpork, most interestingly the Moist von Lipwig books, in which a con-man is put in charge of failing institutions, and *Unseen Academicals*, which contrasts a sport with the working lives of those 'below stairs' at Unseen University. It is also the means – at first as labourers exploited by Harry King, then as skilled workers on the Clacks (the semaphore-signalling system which is the Discworld equivalent of the telegraph or the internet) – by which the goblins gain value and become accepted as 'people'.

CHANGES

In *Reaper Man*, Death encounters Ned Simnel, whose Combination Harvester will render traditional scythes redundant. But his thoughts about 'taking the horse out of the equation' are disrupted by the distraction of a kettle boiling over, extinguishing his fire (*RM* 153). It is not yet 'steam engine time', to use Charles Fort's famous phrase.[16] Later Discworld novels see Ankh-Morpork and its relationships with surrounding countries change from the faux-medieval of much fantasy to an industrial-revolution setting. In part, this is the revival of moribund institutions as Vetinari becomes more established as Patrician and more able to control the city. Reviving the Watch is the first step. *The Truth* brings the printing press to the city. The novel itself parodies Pratchett's own experience as a local journalist, with jokes about 'humorously shaped' vegetables, journalistic clichés and people who believe anything in the paper *must* be true. But it argues the case for a free press, even though 'the truth will make ye fret' (*TT* 129).

Vetinari instigates his own change in *Going Postal*. Moist von Lipwig is offered the choice between being hanged for being a confidence trickster and reforming the post office, driven to near-extinction by the Clacks, which is transforming the nature and tempo of communications. In *Making Money*, Moist is ordered to run the Royal Bank of Ankh-Morpork, and in *Raising Steam* (where Ned Simnel's son Dick brings about 'steam engine time' by inventing the Iron Girder locomotive), he finances the construction of railway lines to Genua and Quirm, and eventually Überwald. As Pratchett and his readers found Discworld an increasingly creative location for stories, the critique of fantasy which was always there in the amused mockery of generic fantasylands implied confrontation and interrogation as well as simple parody. In short, despite the way many post-Tolkienian fantasylands are essentially static locations where the same story is told over and over again – a point underlined in Diana Wynne Jones's *Tough Guide to Fantasyland* where the reader explores genre fantasy's stereotypical worlds in a mock-guidebook – fantasy *can* be used to stimulate and to ask questions. How, one might ask, could a 'fantasyland' develop? How can fantasyland illuminate the world of its readers? Can a fantasy scenario imagine social and individual change? These later novels chart Vetinari's development of Ankh-Morpork and consolidation of its relationships with the outer world in co-operation with Rhys, the Low King of the Dwarfs, Mr Shine, the Troll king, and the Lady Margolotta of Überwald, with whom Vetinari may be having some sort of relationship.

Pratchett's ability to keep at least two major threads interweaving keeps Discworld fresh and inventive. *The Fifth Elephant* shows Vimes, now Duke of Ankh-Morpork, on a diplomatic mission to the vast territory of Überwald where the accession of a new Low King is set to have repercussions in Ankh-Morpork (the largest Dwarf city on Discworld) as well as locally, affecting shifting relationships between Vampires and Werewolves (whose leading family is that of Angua of the Watch). Jokes about diplomats and diplomacy have serious undercurrents, as does the picture of Ankh-Morpork from the point of view of Überwaldians attracted by the economic magnet of a city which wants to exploit its natural resources. Carrot is taken off the scene when he follows Angua, who is still unsure about their relationship, to Überwald, opening space for a more conventional farcical element when Colon is put in charge of the Watch and becomes power-mad and paranoid.

Thud! continues with these diplomatic anxieties, and includes the scenes in which Sam reads *Where's My Cow?* to Young Sam – scenes invoking in turn the conventionality of picture-books for infants, the desperate love Vimes has for his child and – because the story is all about perception – the sudden awareness that he must look at the facts differently to solve his case. *Monstrous Regiment* is a parody of the folk ballads of girls going off to be soldiers. Polly is a native of backward and warlike Borogravia, and the novel, in keeping with its theme of reversal – Polly's fellow-recruits are *also* young women assuming male identity to join the army for various reasons, including escaping institutional abuse – allows us to look at other aspects of Discworld through other eyes. We are given another picture of the less 'civilised' regions of Discworld versus Ankh-Morpork: an imperialist power absorbing the others.

LANDSCAPE

A sense of place is increasingly important in Pratchett's work. This manifests in two ways. The first exploits reader hunger for more of the Discworld, responded to by the maps, calendars and almanacs that add another layer to the imaginary-visual experience. We also see Ankh-Morpork, in the fiction, being given what so many fantasy cities do not have: the sense of a working economy as Vetinari encourages/forces the resurrection of moribund institutions. Technological innovations widen the scope still further. There are still jokes. But they are aimed at different targets, those of a changing *urban* life, requiring postal services, banks and traffic control.

The second manifestation of place is a more 'writerly' development of what Martin Brown, in his survey of Discworld's archaeological features, calls the 'relationships and the layers which build up a landscape and a place'.[17] Tiffany Aching's homeland is similar to the Wiltshire Pratchett moved to in 1993, 'full of tiny, intricate flowers, like cowslips and harebells, and even smaller ones that somehow survived the grazing' (*WFM* 13). Here too we have ancient stone circles and barrows. In the Discworld's Chalk (as in the chalk downs of south England), there are hills associated with stories about dragons and buried kings, there are megaliths, fossils and fossil-like strangely shaped flints, figures carved into the chalk. The White Horse of Uffington is the source for the carving in *A Hat Full of Sky* and the pendant which, in that novel, Roland gives Tiffany and which plays a significant part in *Wintersmith*. The Cerne Abbas Giant is the source for the hill-figure at the scouring fair in *I Shall Wear Midnight* whose 'lack of trousers filled the world' (*ISWM* 12).

Pratchett's deep vein of folklore creates an imagined past for the Discworld. Some of it is there for its humorous effect. Barrows in Lancre attract their own version of the folklore about leaving your unshod horse and a sixpence in payment for fairy smiths: 'in the morning the sixpence would be gone and you'd never see your horse again, either' (*CJ* 191). The standing stone in *Wyrd Sisters* is, like the Rollright Stones in Oxfordshire, uncountable (despite there being only one of it). Other monuments reveal deeper and more symbolic aspects of landscape. The Long Man, two round and one long burial mound, is the very picture of 'the landscape saying: I've got a great big tonker' (*LL* 218). Beneath it is a chambered tomb containing slabs arranged in a spiral (a significant neolithic symbol) and an unnamed king and his warriors sleeping, as do Arthur and his men, until their country needs them.[18] Even beyond this is the horned Elf-king with all the attributes the landscape suggests and who Nanny Ogg threatens with the traditional menace of iron shovels excavating his barrows, transforming legend into dull archaeological accounts of 'just an old earthworks' (*LL* 224). Folklorish significance of 'hollow hills' makes barrows the home of the Nac Mac Feegle. The Kelda, the ruler (and mother) of the Feegle unit in *Carpe Jugulum*, is described in terms of figures such as the Upper Paeleolithic (c. 29,500 years BP) Venus of Willendorf: 'exactly like the little figurines back in the days of ice and mammoths' (*CJ* 191).

Also significant in the Lancre landscape is the stone circle, the Dancers, a name evoking the Cornish Merry Maidens and other monuments in the British landscape.[19] *Lords and Ladies* begins with young Esmerelda Weatherwax tempted to cross the boundary between the worlds of Elves and humans. The Dancers act as a barrier between worlds, but are also a portal which, once triggered, allows the entry of supernatural beings like the unicorn, and the Elves themselves. The double-vision of barrier/portal reflects the double-vision of fantasy, the mode which allows us to see the familiar and the estranging reacting and intertwining together.

THE DISCWORLD 'MAP'

It is possible to consider the Discworld series, with its recurring characters and settings, as if not a unified mega-novel, certainly a mosaic repaying consideration as a whole. Its variations of tone, setting and character circle around some deep and occasionally troubling questions about how we as individuals and societies construct ourselves. Evidence from the texts, and comments from Pratchett in articles and interviews, suggests that this was not so much a planned project as an exploration or discovery as new ideas came to him and as Discworld was, despite the disclaimer in *Sourcery*, mapped.

Unfinished ideas and drafts were famously crushed under the wheel of a steamroller after Pratchett's death,[20] but evidence of this ad hoc development can be seen in the way Pratchett (as Lawrence Watt-Evans observes) operates by 'taking some bit of business and moving it from one character to another',[21] filing off the rough edges as necessary. In *The Colour of Magic*, Rincewind entertains what Twoflower calls the 'fantasy' of thinking that the world should be more logical and organised. In interest of establishing him as the Eternal Coward, Rincewind loses this curiosity, which is then attached to Mort before becoming fixed into Ponder Stibbons and his High Energy Magic Team. In *Equal Rites*, the literal-minded Zoons appear and vanish, apart from a footnoted reference in *Snuff*, to have some of their characteristics transferred to the Dwarfs, and Hilta Goatfinder similarly 'vanishes' to become, in part, Nanny Ogg. In *Thud!*, the vampire Sally, a new Watch recruit, joins Angua as a cloud of bats. Returning to her human form, she is naked. The plot issue raised by Angua, remembering another vampire character who could rematerialise *his* clothes, is resolved by a hand-waving explanation that female vampires just *can't*: 'We don't know why. It's probably part of the whole underwired nightdress business' (*Th* 171). *Reaper Man* refers to a 'glib bugger in [...] red and yellow tights' who rids Ankh-Morpork of a plague of rats, although it is unclear whether Mr so-called Amazing Maurice is actually the cat of *The Amazing Maurice and His Educated Rodents*, set in the wilder region of Überwald and which develops the Pied Piper story into an extended slapstick routine on Pratchett's favourite topics of story and ethics.

Not all of this 'business' necessarily works. Jokes and situations, such as frequent loss of bladder control in situations of fear or stress, can be overused. The use in *Maurice* of a Kenneth Williams catchphrase from the 1950s BBC radio series *Hancock's Half Hour* and *Beyond Our Ken* is rather too obviously aimed at adult readers who remember Williams's snide delivery. Vetinari's channelling of the comedy-magician Tommy Cooper in *Jingo* seems to clash with the Patrician's character, though other readings of this scene might see it as deliberately inverting the formal and focused persona with which he rules Ankh-Morpork.

The power-supplying Devices discovered deep underground by the Dwarfs in *Thud!*, which might even predate the Discworld, echo the Thing which guides the Nomes in the Bromeliad trilogy and seem to resurrect ideas from Pratchett's pre-Discworld science fiction novels. Whether this was a seed which was eventually to turn a fantasy series towards a new direction, or simply a playful re-use of an idea, is, after Pratchett's death, a question hardly worth posing, except that it does show Pratchett constantly pushing his creation, refining his craft. Reading Discworld in this way shows how Pratchett's imagination, fuelled by his omnivorous reading and massive sense of curiosity, constantly worked. Discworld is one of the very few cases of lengthy series, certainly in the fantasy/sf fields where later books are better than earlier ones, which have not decayed into wooden facsimiles of earlier successes.

4

Outside Discworld: The Non-series Works

While still developing Discworld at pace – sometimes two novels a year – Pratchett soon developed side-projects such as *The Unadulterated Cat*, illustrated by Gray Jolliffe, and the collaboration with Neil Gaiman, *Good Omens*, later a successful TV series. He also produced separate series and stand-alone novels, where he could allow his moral analysis and character-based humour free flow in environments other than Discworld and show that he was more than a one-trick writer. In doing so, he was also able to extend and explore his abilities in ways which made later Discworld books richer. In *The Unadulterated Cat*, the character analysis of the 'real cat' in what is essentially an extended newspaper column spoof on the problems of cat ownership (however funny), later enriched *The Amazing Maurice and His Educated Rodents*. The Johnny Maxwell series allowed him to develop another fictional location (the town of Blackbury) first imagined in his Uncle Jim children's stories for the *Bucks Free Press*. The Bromeliad trilogy extended the 'little people' motifs of *The Carpet People* and some of his early *Bucks Free Press* stories, and *Nation* and *Dodger* were more realistic alternative-history experiments.

GOOD OMENS: WILLIAM THE ANTICHRIST

Good Omens began in 1985 with a scenario written by Gaiman in which Richmal Crompton's William becomes the Antichrist.[1] Pratchett eventually suggested that the pair develop it, and the novel was eventually published in 1990. Two main strands eventually formed *Good Omens*: the relationship between the angel Aziraphale and the demon Crowley, and the rise of the Antichrist to his full power in the Last Days leading up to the Apocalypse – where, unfortunately, the baby destined to *be* the Antichrist has been delivered to the wrong parents. These strands are linked by the relationship between Anathema Device, descendant of the witch Agnes Nutter whose Nice and Accurate Prophecies chart (in frequently confusing detail) events since her death in the seventeenth century, and trainee Witchfinder Newton Pulsifer, descendant of the man who executed Agnes.

Aziraphale and Crowley, since the Fall and the Expulsion of Adam and Eve from Eden, have allowed their relationship as adversaries to cosy into a working arrangement. Each covers for the other where necessary, making the novel a morality play questioning the notion of good and evil. Crowley, tasked to promote evil, is nonplussed when credited for horrors that the human race has devised without any demonic intervention, and amazed by humanity's capacity for grace. Aziraphale, who gave his flaming sword to Adam and Eve because the pair needed warmth and protection outside Eden, cannot commit himself to embracing the necessity for a Final Conflict. Each, in their different ways, is comfortable with Earthly existence. But *Good Omens* is not only replaying the script of the Apocalypse. It is replaying the story of the Fall. The Antichrist, through a series of mishaps and blunders on the part of the demons overseeing his Earthly incarnation, is now named Adam and grows up in an Edenic English village where he is tempted to turn the world into a solipsistic Paradise for small boys: endless 'cowboys and indians' games, entire continents for his friends to rule, and no rules whatsoever about bedtimes, healthy foods or going to school. But Adam comes to understand that the real world is wonderful and interesting, that allowing it to be destroyed in a nuclear holocaust so that it can be rebuilt is perhaps over the top, and that the best thing about play is that you can stop and go home. When Death and Beelzebub tell him that his fate as the Antichrist is written, Adam's response is that he has not yet exhausted the magic of the world. What is written can always be crossed out. He resists temptation because while the Horsemen of the Apocalypse are his kind of people (supernatural entities),

Pepper, Wensley and Brian, the 'Them', are his *real* friends and, as ordinary humans, his kind of people too.

Both Pratchett and Gaiman dealt with the questionable morality enshrined in theology in their individual works – Gaiman in the figure of Lucifer in his Sandman series and Pratchett in novels like *Small Gods* – but *Good Omens* enabled each to rework the other's ideas. While the larger part of the text seems to have been written by Pratchett – partly because Gaiman was tied to the strict timetable of his regular Sandman comic-book series – and the novel's footnotes follow standard Pratchettian practice, the authors' afterwords to the Corgi 2006 edition describe an intense process of revision and rewriting. This was followed through to the point where Pratchett added an extra scene to the US edition at the request of an American editor who wanted more about a particular (American) character. This change was then incorporated into the British paperback reprint.[2] *Good Omens* is perhaps a sidebar in Pratchett's career, but, thanks in part due to the success of the Amazon/BBC television series starring David Tennant and Michael Sheen (2019, 2023), in which Gaiman developed some of the vaguely sketched ideas for a sequel, it is a rewarding one.

THE BROMELIAD: POCKET UNIVERSE

At a sales conference in 1988, the then children's editor of Corgi asked Pratchett if he would consider writing for children.[3] The result was the Nomes or Bromeliad series: *Truckers*, *Diggers* and *Wings*. Four-inch-high beings living in a department store which is being closed down discover that they are the descendants of space-travellers who have crash-landed on Earth. The Bromeliad trilogy is a classic, if unusual 'Pocket Universe' science fiction situation in which people leave a closed environment and learn that the 'world' is much bigger.[4] When Masklin and his companions escape their hostile environment and enter the Store, they disrupt the constricted and inward-looking assumption of the Store nomes that the Store is all there is, created for them by 'Arnold Bros (est. 1905)', who has established the Store and all in it for their benefit. While many Pocket Universe stories, such as Robert A. Heinlein's 'Universe' (1951) and Brian Aldiss's

Non-Stop (1958) feature such situations as descendants of starship crews rediscovering the fact that the starship is *not* the entire universe, Pratchett's setting is close to Mary Norton's Borrowers sequence (1952–1982), in which small people dwell behind the walls of a house and, like the Bromeliad's nomes, live off what they can scavenge from the larger 'human' inhabitants.

Echoes of Discworld exist in the way store departments are translated into the Italian Renaissance names of nomes tribes (Haberdasheri, Ironmongri, Del Icatessen) recalling Vetinari, and in some of the characters. Granny Morkie is a somewhat diluted Granny Weatherwax. The trilogy's roots go back into the way Pratchett's own life was influenced by his childhood reading. Childhood is a matter of continual development, of coming to understand that the world (and the self) is more complicated, and more wondrous, than it seems. For the nomes, the apparently static childlike model, and the religion and code of ethics built up around Arnold Bros (est. 1905) is disrupted when Masklin, Grimma, Granny Morkie and the others, bearing a talisman of uncertain function they call the Thing, arrive from an Outside which, according to dogma, does not exist. Pratchett plays amusingly and thoughtfully with the conceptual breakthroughs that follow.

Taking the closing-down sale slogan 'Everything Must Go' as a literal warning of the end of the world, the nomes must rebuild not only their relationship with the Store and their 'god' but the wider universe from which their ancestors came. In *Truckers*, Masklin, with the help of the Thing, revealed as a Flight Navigation and Recording Computer awakened by contact with electricity in the Store, leads the nomes escape from the Store's demolition by hijacking a truck, driving it by means of a complicated system of ropes and levers. The disused quarry to which they flee is, they discover in *Diggers*, to be re-opened, but a nearby airport offers the possibility of an aeroplane journey to Florida, where the Thing can hijack the launch of a communications satellite and contact a mothership waiting on the moon. Masklin and two others make the transatlantic journey while Grimma remains to help the Store nomes deal with human intrusion. *Wings* tells how Masklin, Gurder and Angalo travel to Florida, discovering other nomes who have constructed their own religion out of the 'Maker of Clouds' or NASA.

Pratchett's jokes echo the bewilderment of children in a world adults are often unable or unwilling to explain. The exchanges between the Store nomes and Masklin's 'outsiders' are full of misunderstandings and cross-purposes. Nomes understand explanations literally, without comprehending context. For example, stars are clearly very far away, but how far is difficult to understand: 'Even if you ran all the way, it'd probably take weeks to reach them' (*Tr* 107). Fiction and reality are blurred. Much of the nomes' ability to decipher the truth about their world comes from understanding (or *mis*understanding, for this is after all, a comedy) the information they discover in books. The *Highway Code* gives instructions about driving – but not actually about *how* to drive, and especially not about how a team of four-inch high nomes might control a vehicle. Faced with the question of how to escape from the Store and return to their own realm, the nomes invent Critical Path Analysis. Their task is a massive, almost impossible one, but by stripping it down into smaller sub-tasks they achieve it.

As with children's education, each small addition to knowledge clears up an area of ignorance only to reveal another expanse of wider ignorance. This is shown in *Diggers* in the image which gives the trilogy its title, when Masklin and Grimma argue. This is partly because Masklin simply assumes that they should get together as a couple. Grimma, though, wants something more. Learning to read *is*, as the Abbot warns, dangerous. It *does* (albeit metaphorically) make women's heads explode. Grimma reads about 'Southamerica', where there are

> great big flowers called bromeliads and water gets into the flowers and makes little pools and there's a type of frog that lays eggs in the pools and tadpoles hatch and grow into new frogs and these little frogs live their whole lives in the flowers right at the top of the trees and don't even know about the ground and the world is full of things like that and now I know about them and I'm never ever going to be able to see them and then you [...] want me to come and live with you in a hole and wash your socks! (*Di* 42)

This image continues throughout *Diggers* and *Wings* until Masklin, reflecting upon the changes in his life, realises that '[o]nce you know things, you're a different person. You can't help it' (*Wi* 100–101).

As Peter Hunt remarks, the underlying premise of small people 'in a world governed by big people to whom they cannot relate and who they can scarcely understand' is a metaphor for childhood, but the single image throughout *Wings* of the frogs living their entire lives within flowers in the South American treetop canopy shifts the series towards a greater metaphor of 'transcending boundaries whether or not you really know that they are there'.[5]

JOHNNY MAXWELL: TRYING TIMES

The Johnny Maxwell series for children, *Only You Can Save Mankind*, *Johnny and the Dead* and *Johnny and the Bomb*, is more realistic (in the sense that the characters are young people in a recognisable twentieth-century England), but it also deals with different versions of the fantastic. The setting is the semi-fantastic Blackbury, of many of the early newspaper stories and the location of the Arnold Bros store in the Bromeliad books). In the first novel, Johnny, living through the 'trying times' of his parents' marital difficulties, discovers that the aliens he enthusiastically destroys in his computer shoot-'em-up game are real. In the second, the sale of Blackbury's cemetery affects the ghosts of people buried there, who are to be re-buried elsewhere. In the third and most complicated novel, Johnny and his friends are enabled, through the mysterious squishy bags in the trolley belonging to the curiously long-lived and eccentric Mrs Tachyon, to travel back to Blackbury's wartime past to prevent the bombing of a street.

In the trilogy, Pratchett 'takes on the huge and solemn genre of the teenage problem novel' and carries out 'a thorough demolition of the cliches of children's fantasy'[6] in ways more subversive than simple mockery. Johnny and his friends are misfits. Wobbler is fat, a computer geek and a coward who, given the chance in the alternative 'trouser of time' in which he finds himself in *Johnny and the Bomb*, grows up to be a successful businessman. Bigmac is a skinhead yob from the wrong part of town and the wrong kind of family but is a mathematical genius. Yo-less, who wants to be a doctor and a lawyer, is black, and resolutely uncool with none of the stereotypical traits of 'black youth'. Kirsty is a high-achieving feminist who comes across as egotistical, even rude, but, as Cherith Baldry points out, by the end of the novel she has clearly shown commitment to the others 'even though she might not admit it'.[7] Apart from Johnny she is the only one to remember their experiences in wartime Blackbury, suggesting a mental flexibility comparable to Johnny's own.

Johnny's own 'trying times' means that he must often fend for himself for meals and laundry. In *Only You Can Save Mankind*, he faints at Kirsty's house and her mother is clearly concerned about him. His parents have actually split in *Johnny and the Dead*, when he and his mother are living with his grandfather, and in *Johnny and the Bomb* Johnny is carrying home notes from school saying that he is clinically 'disturbed'. Yet the sequence is a successful comedy, partly because it inverts the hushed piousness with which teenage problems can be discussed. Johnny's friends tease him because of his 'madness': 'Now personally I think you're very nearly totally disturbed and suffering from psycho-somatica and hearing voices and seeing delusions'. But they *support* him. 'that doesn't matter, 'cos we're friends' (*JATD* 46). Johnny's detachment – on one level, *Only You Can Save Mankind* is about a boy escaping into computer games – does not prevent him from developing empathy for the ScreeWee whose destiny is to be eliminated by the game's players. He urges his friends, in *Johnny and the Dead*, to take seriously the anxiety of the 'inhabitants' of Blackbury Cemetery when it is sold to a development company. We need the memories of the past to 'tell us who we are' (*JATD* 114). In *Johnny and the Bomb*, he organises the rescue of Mrs Tachyon when she is found injured, visits her in hospital, and quickly recognises the difference between her apparently incoherent 'eccentricity' and the logic of 'sane' people who drop bombs on streets of civilians.

Pratchett also undercuts the cosiness of children's adventure books where plucky youngsters defeat crooks and wicked bureaucrats. Property developers are always an easy target, and with that in mind, *Johnny and the Dead* is perhaps the most conventional children's story, with the obvious enemy being the conglomerate who have bought the graveyard for fivepence. But it is an adult, Mr Atterbury, who is clever (and able) enough to defeat the company's plans once Johnny's questions at the public meeting give him the opening. In *Johnny and the Bomb*, Kirsty casts herself as one of Enid Blyton's Famous Five, a classic children's adventure-series: 'Me, and four token boys […] It's only a mercy we haven't got a dog' (*JATB* 73–74). Pratchett himself is typically sardonic about the desperate liberalism in many such texts. Bigmac respects the social worker who makes it clear that he should be 'strangled at birth. You could respect someone like that. They didn't make you feel like some kind of useless nerd' (*JATB* 94). The Dead inhabiting Blackbury cemetery are caricatures, including a Marxist atheist who refuses to believe in such nonsense as afterlives, but there is humour and truth in their positioning as the past which must be remembered in order to give meaning to the present, in the repartee between the children themselves and in Pratchett's sly inserts from an 'adult' viewpoint such as the Gulf War, at its height when *Only You Can Save Mankind* was written and published, experienced by the children as a version of their computer shoot-em-up games. One of the humourless and unimaginative Councillors in *Johnny and the Dead* is a descendant of the Dead idealistic suffragette Sylvia Liberty. There is a library that is 'so new it didn't even have librarians. It had Assistant Information Officers' (*JATD* 68).

The 'engine' of the series, however, is the moral impetus behind it. 'Everything you do changes everything' (*JATB* 189). The multiverse of possible futures becomes Johnny's guide to do the right thing rather than a way of adjusting plot, as the children find in *Johnny and the Bomb* when they discover that they *can* change the course of events so that nineteen people do not die.

LONG EARTH: STEPPING OUT

At a dinner-party in early 2010, Pratchett mentioned to sf writer Stephen Baxter 'The High Meggas', planned to be a series following *The Colour of Magic*, but put aside when Discworld became popular. Pratchett wrote *The Light Fantastic* instead, and the original story was not published until the collection of short fiction *A Blink on the Screen*. Baxter, one of Britain's leading sf writers in the tradition of Arthur C. Clarke, with whom he had earlier collaborated in *The Light of Other Days* and the Time Odyssey trilogy (2003–07), agreed to collaborate on two novels, although the series spread to five: *The Long Earth. The Long War, The Long Mars, The Long Utopia* and *The Long Cosmos*.

The first novel in the series begins with a soldier from the First World War stepping into another Earth inhabited by humanoids, and with fifteen-year-old Maria Valienté giving birth to baby Joshua on another parallel Earth. It follows with details of 'step' machines publicly released by a mysterious scientist, Willis Linsay, resulting in a 'mass stepping' causing panic. Many of the 'steppers' do not really understand what they are doing and where they are going. Joshua Valienté, brought up in an orphanage run by nuns, becomes famous for helping lost steppers to return, but stepping also opens up the chance for people to abandon their mundane lives and establish communities in parallel Earths. The following novels continue the story with a range of characters including Joshua, Linsay and his daughter Sally, Nelson Azikiwe, a South African priest, and Lobsang, an artificial intelligence who claims to be the reincarnation of a Tibetan motorcycle repairman. Lobsang and Joshua begin the first of a series of voyages across multiple worlds either side of what comes to be called Datum Earth. Subsequent novels explore the range of life forms across the Long Earth, especially the numerous humanoid species dubbed trolls, elves and kobolds. *The Long Mars* shows how the discovery/revelation of stepping has accelerated the development of a super-intelligent sub-race who call themselves the Next. The mystery of how and why stepping has developed in modern humanity is revealed in *The Long Utopia*, which also reveals Joshua's ancestry.

The series draws upon the strengths of two writers who are known for their incisive and inventive imaginations in rather different branches of science fiction. It is an imaginative sequence, marred by plot holes, and the sometimes-random appearance and disappearance of characters. In *The Long Utopia* Joshua wonders why Willis Linsay, who has played a major part in the previous novel, is not present. His daughter's reply, 'If he wanted to be here, he would be' (*TLU* 339), seems less an answer than an authorial attempt to cover the gap. The final novel, offering a cosmic structure of a 'Skein' of 'long' worlds weaving in and out of each other, brings the saga to a close with the introduction of an alien race of Traversers, but fails to explain – and tells us that it does not explain – the meaning of inscriptions on the monoliths discovered in *The Long Mars*. Much of these discontinuities are caused by the need to complete the series during and after Pratchett's illness, but they mean that the series does not stand alongside Pratchett's major achievements. It is less for the general readership Pratchett was developing than an entertainment for the science fiction fan who will understand the references to Isaac Asimov, Frank Herbert, Kim Stanley Robinson and others. *The Long Cosmos*, with its Clarke Project and space-pod named Uncle Arthur, is clearly – whether through Baxter or Pratchett's influence or more likely both – an homage to Arthur C. Clarke, especially the visionary Clarke of *Childhood's End* (1953), *The City and the Stars* (1956) and *2001: A Space Odyssey* (1968). Only occasionally does the series approach the visionary nature which Pratchett clearly attended.

HISTORICAL OTHERWORLDS: *NATION* AND *DODGER*

In his acceptance speech for the 2009 Boston Globe-Horn Book Fiction Award for *Nation*, Pratchett described it as 'the best book I have ever written or will write' (*ASOTK* 141). Mau, a Pacific Islands boy, is about to undergo the ceremonies that will make him a man when a massive tsunami destroys his people. He and Daphne, a young English girl shipwrecked by the tsunami upon Mau's island, are in some ways typical Pratchett characters– young people determined to understand the world they live in. This leads to incongruities and misunderstandings, but, while 'humour does break out sometimes in the book' (*ASOTK* 141), it is by no means a comedy. According to the customs of his people, Mau does not know how to be a man, yet finds himself in the role of leader as scattered survivors converge upon his island. Daphne (christened Ermintrude) has been schooled in how to be a 'young lady' by her grandmother, but she has her own tragedy: the death of her mother in childbirth. The burial of the baby in a separate coffin haunts her with the sense that it will be lonely without its mother.

Nation is set in an alternative nineteenth century. William Whiting's hymn 'Eternal Father, Strong to Save', written in 1860 and a reference to the recent Crimean War (1853–1856), offer clues to dates, but Pratchett juggles history and geography to give his world a Reunited States, an Australia of two islands, and its own fauna and flora (the 'lonesome palm' and the 'sailfin crocodile'). There are echoes of Discworld in theme and character. *Nation*'s tension between science and religion is one of Pratchett's recurrent motifs. A foul-mouthed parrot is reminiscent of that in *Eric*. Unsurprisingly perhaps, Locaha the god of death speaks like his Discworld counterpart. But *Nation* stands on its own, carefully crafted. Maria Błaszkiewicz considers it a novel of reversal, with its astonishing opening scene as the Sweet Judy is carried across the island's rainforest with its half-mad Captain extemporising new verses to Whiting's hymn to add 'on the land' to the famous plea to guard 'those in peril on the sea'. This sets up a number of responses to the idea of the 'ship of state', reworking a rather stale allegory 'by means of a characteristic mixture of seriousness, even earnestness, with irony and dark humour'.[8] Captain Roberts's last thoughts are among Pratchett's finest (and most self-revealing) examples of this mixture: facing the inevitable end, he tinkers with a line in his verse to substitute a more appropriate and euphonic word. The wreck of the Judy becomes, like Robinson Crusoe's ship, a treasure-house of resources for the Islanders as they rebuild their society, but there is an ironic undercurrent. The tools of the 'trousermen' (European sailors) are recognised by the priest Ataba as carrying their own threat of exploitation. 'It starts with knives and cooking pots, and suddenly [...] our souls do not belong to us' (*N* 256). The more metaphorical 'shipwreck' of the British state – a maritime Empire where a virulent 'Russian influenza' has wiped out the British Royal family and 137 heirs – opens up room for a compromise engineered by Pratchett's alternative-history setting but which offers hope just as Mau and Daphne's world-maps are overturned by their experiences.

Mau is troubled by contradictions within a religion that implies a personal involvement by a god or gods who are nowhere when disaster strikes their people. The debate between Mau and Ataba, himself anguished by his inability to understand why Mau's sister, or his own daughter and grandchildren were allowed to die, but who retains his 'belief', is not one between enemies. It is the mutineer Cox – like *Night Watch's* Carcer a sociopath who 'turns people into creatures like himself' (*N* 320) – who is the real incarnation of evil. Daphne – who comes to understand that her grandmother's veneration of Ancestors is little different from the Islander's consciousness of the need to propitiate Grandfathers – is also able to deduce from the evidence of her and Mau's exploration that the Nation was, long ago, an advanced civilisation. This twist is one found in various sf novels of dubious merit, but is carried off by Pratchett, who allows Mau's and Daphne's changing world-views to offer a solution to the dilemma posed by Ataba. The Nation will accept the Empire's knowledge, but not its political domination. The compact survives because it is brokered by two people who think more about their people than themselves.

Dodger is broadly (Pratchett deliberately tweaked the historical record to allow some of his characters to be present at the same time) a historical novel. It draws upon the factual records of Henry Mayhew, author of *London Labour and the London Poor* (1851) and the fiction of Charles Dickens, which crystallises in the figure of Dodger, an artful young 'tosher', or scavenger in the noxious London sewers, who rescues a young woman escaping an abusive marriage to a German prince, and is aided by Dickens and Mayhew.

If Discworld allows Pratchett to take an imaginary location and set it growing as an otherworld, in *Nation* and *Dodger* he is able to move away from Discworld to express his moral debates in settings less familiar to his readers. In *Dodger*, particularly, he exploits his wide reading outside sf, especially of Victorian London's metaphorical and literal underworld. Perhaps because they were aimed at young adults, Pratchett's voice in these novels avoids much of Discworld's in-jokes about what his readers know. Instead, he is careful to share a kind of sense of wonder as he reveals what they almost certainly *don't* know but what he has discovered in his research. It is significant that it is Dickens the journalist who is important in *Dodger*. The 'truth', as de Worde also discovers in the Discworld novel, is always a fog out of which 'journalists, as mere wielders of the pen, have to distil [...] such truths that mankind, not being godlike, can understand' (*Do* 135). Here we have Pratchett's own experience as a journalist peeking out, even as the aspiring novelist scribbles down titles for novels from random phrases in conversation. Discworld worked and developed, perhaps, because Pratchett was ambitious to expand his horizons as a writer. As a science fiction and fantasy reader he had seen too many series crumble into repetition. In moving away from Discworld, he proved that he was capable of independent work while the original setting grew more flexible as his abilities to pull humour out of character grew. Pratchett argued, in his Carnegie Medal Award speech, that *The Amazing Maurice* was 'quite a serious book. Only the scenery is funny'.[9] The following chapters will suggest how Pratchett engaged with 'serious' themes which, in the hands of a lesser writer, would overbalance with solemnity or be lost in bathos.

5

Pratchett and the 'Cauldron of Story'

J. R. R. Tolkien's essay 'On Fairy-stories' tells us about the forever-boiling 'Cauldron of Story'[1] from which we pluck characters, themes and motifs. This is not the taxonomical cataloguing which, since Antii Aarne, Stith Thompson and Vladimir Propp, analyses folk tales. Nor is it Joseph Campbell's Jungian 'monomyth' knowingly employed by George Lucas in the *Star Wars* series.[2] Nor is it even, exactly, the survival of half-forgotten myth or the opposite 'rise' of local heroes to become mythic archetypes. Instead, Tolkien describes elements, such as the character Bertha Broadfoot (the mother of Charlemagne), and episodes of the story collected in the nineteenth century by the Brothers Grimm in 'The Goose-Girl', elements 'cast into the simmering stew'[3] to emerge combined as stories.

This is a useful if not entirely comprehensive metaphor for how writers work: mining stores of possible stories in search of a combination of reader recognition and originality. John Clute, in the *Encyclopedia of Fantasy*, uses both 'Cauldron of Story' and 'Ocean of Story' to express the sense that '[a]lmost every traditional STORY exists in multiple versions'.[4] Tolkien himself points out that such employment of basic elements does not mean that any two or more stories built from these elements are the same story – an error, he says, folklorists are particularly prone to. What we might call story-events become attached to an individual. Or, as it might be, the other way around: individuals become attached to stories already told about others and become 'new bits added to the stock', new ways of telling stories already told.[5]

It is sometimes useful also to see genres as 'essentially contracts between a writer and [...] readers'.[6] Farah Mendlesohn writes that '[o]ver the past seventy years the community of sf writers has developed a tool kit', consisting of 'the evolution of a vocabulary, of a structure and a set of shared ideas [...] deeply embedded in the genre's psyche'.[7] There, writing about science fiction, much of what she has to say is applicable to fantasy (she expands her analysis in *Rhetorics of Fantasy*, where she talks about Pratchett's use of 'legacy texts' and reader-expectation),[8] and the by no means univocal community of writers and readers engaged in both genres during the twentieth century (of whom Pratchett, of course, was one). This consensus allowed sf writer and critic Damon Knight to argue in 1952 that sf 'means what we point to when we say it',[9] the point being that Knight himself could indicate a 'we' with a shared understanding of the vocabulary and story-patterns comprising what 'we' point to. Terry Pratchett's audience began among a particular community: British sf and fantasy readers, convention goers and fans. His success took him to new audiences: children and more general readers who may not have shared his original legacy texts, but who responded to and were encouraged to understand his omnivorous reading and use of the 'cauldron of story'.

Pratchett is neither a cataloguer, nor a psychologist, or the kind of fantasy writer exemplified by Alan Garner, for whom myth is a set of resonating patterns which, in *The Owl Service* (1967) or *Red Shift* (1973), arise and repeat like motifs in a musical score.[10] Although, as a humourist, he might not be taking 'faerie', the realm of fantasy, as seriously as Tolkien might like, he is as a storyteller equally drawing upon the 'cauldron'/ 'soup' of story. His own description of his technique is less dependent on culinary metaphor, although in one interview he remarks that 'Fantasy is not the icing on the cake, Fantasy is the whole cake'.[11] His term 'white knowledge' – 'the sort of stuff that fills up your brain without you really knowing where it came from' – evokes 'white noise' – radio static or noise containing all frequencies equally across the audible spectrum, and is also, in another culinary reference, the 'sea of undigested information' in which we swim.[12] It is what 'a generally well-read (well-viewed, well-listened) person has a sporting chance of picking up'.[13] If Pratchett does not identify motifs as an act of scholarship, he assumes his readers recognise patterns when they read them. Just as we may not be expected to identify all the classical/Shakespearian allusions P. G. Wodehouse's Bertie Wooster misremembers or fails to understand, so Pratchett hardly relies on all readers understanding all his references. But while some readers of *Witches Abroad* might not recognise 'some ole enchantress in history who lived on an island and turned shipwrecked sailors into pigs' or why a 'voodoo' deity might be 'Mr Safe Way' (a complicated multilingual pun on supermarket names involving the importance of crossroads), they might immediately understand the allusion in 'You know, Greebo', she said, 'I don't think we're in Lancre' (*WA* 118, 9, 123). For an immediate encounter with the range of 'white knowledge' and intertextual borrowing within a Pratchett novel, Darryl Jones and David Lloyd's notes to the Penguin Modern Classics edition of *Night Watch* are helpful and entertaining. Throughout his novels, Pratchett is writing for readers who know how story works, and who enjoy the entanglement of known, or half-remembered, story-elements. Allusions missed at one reading may be understood later, as the reader returns having supped more from the cauldron of story. It is this pleasure of recognition which makes Pratchett so re-readable.

PRATCHETT'S CAULDRON

The European fairy-tale tradition, embodying folk-wisdom and wonder handed down through generations in numerous variant oral or literary retellings, pervades Discworld, as recognised by Kevin Paul Smith in *The Postmodern Fairytale*. Because many readers remember at least the bones of these common-stock stories, they serve as sources for jokes (because they can be easily and recognisably parodied), as recognisable motifs or allusions, and as sources for darker ironies.

Fairy tales infuse the modern fantastic through the late seventeenth-century retellings of Charles Perrault and the Victorian passion for fairies together with the nineteenth-century folk-tale rediscovery of the great collector/editors such as the Grimm brothers, Joseph Jacobs or Andrew Lang. Collectors investigating national folk traditions rediscovered bawdy and sadistic elements. Versions of some of these are hinted at in Granny Weatherwax's refusal in *Witches Abroad* to hear anything about the symbolism of maypoles and witches' broomsticks, and in *Hogfather*, where an archaic side of our jovial Father Christmas is suggested. In the nineteenth century, creative inventors and re-tellers like Hans Christian Andersen encouraged invention of original fantasies. The long tradition of literary adaptation, subversion and playful experimentation includes much of Dickens, Lewis Carroll, George MacDonald, E. Nesbit, J. M. Barrie and L Frank Baum's Oz series, as well as the nineteenth-century popular science-educators such as Arabella Buckley, who used fairy story as a useful metaphor for teaching science to children.[14] As Kevin Smith, analysing modern incorporation of fairy tale, says, 'the fairytale has been used as an intertext' in literally thousands of literary texts.[15] Pratchett is therefore working, as author and moralist, in a long tradition of adaptation and satire of fairy tale. Well aware of how even the most complex narratives fall back upon fairy-tale structures, he keeps them alive as sources for reworkings and retellings. This is particularly the case in *Witches Abroad*, whose heritage includes 'Cinderella', 'Sleeping Beauty', 'Puss in Boots' and *The Wizard of Oz*. In doing so, his work 'addresses the nature of the myths we live by and the fantasies that govern our daily existence'.[16]

More specifically, Pratchett's 'cauldron' also includes, at least in his early works, post-Tolkienian fantasy. Pratchett notes in an interview that he began Discworld as an antidote to 'all the third or fourth hand copies of Tolkien'.[17] By the time of the publication of the first two Discworld books, numerous secondary-world fantasies had achieved success, including the first Shannara trilogy by Terry Brooks (1977–1985) and the five books of David Eddings's Belgariad (1982–1984). Although some of the post-*LOTR* fantasy wave, such as Stephen R. Donaldson's Thomas Covenant, the Unbeliever series (1977–1979 and 1980–1983), were more active critical engagements with the implications of Tolkien's creation, the popularity of Dungeons and Dragons role-playing games and spin-offs such as Margaret Weiss and Tracy Hickman's Dragonlance Chronicles (1984–1985) led to a common acceptance of scenarios involving Elves, Dwarves and Halflings, and quests to defeat a Dark Lord. While Discworld quickly turned from straightforward parody of this generic Fantasyworld (given its own travel-guide in Diana Wynne Jones's *Tough Guide to*

Fantasyland), we still recognise many of its features. The jokes about the difficulty the bearded, reticent dwarfs have with recognising each other's gender are implicit in Tolkien's dwarf women 'so like to the dwarf-men that the eyes and ears of other peoples cannot tell them apart'.[18] In *Witches Abroad*, the 'small grey creature, vaguely froglike, paddling towards them on a log' is gifted by the reference to its 'birthday' to those who remember Smeagol/Gollum's discovery of the Ring in Tolkien's *The Hobbit* (WA 52).

As an avid reader and active convention-going science fiction fan during the 1960s, Pratchett would have also shared in the comprehensive 'Cauldron of Story' known to his fellows. Lovecraft in particular lends himself to the kind of affectionately knowing bathos applied to *Macbeth* at the beginning of *Wyrd Sisters*, where 'When shall we three meet again?' is answered by 'Well, I can do next Tuesday' (WS 5). In *Moving Pictures*, a wizard attempts to investigate a recently slain monstrosity, to be warned, in the words of Lovecraft's 'mad poet' Abdul Alhazred (from 'The Nameless City'):

'That is not dead which can eternal lie'.

[...]

'It looks bloody dead to me', he said. (MP 255–256)

Such quotations form part of the 'undigested information' of catchphrases in a 'generally well-read' sf/fantasy readership.[19] Other allusions are more obliquely intertextual. Introducing *Guilty of Literature*, David Langford suggests that *Pyramids* – in part a compendium of 'all we know about Ancient Egypt' jokes, and including a very fine parody of the scene in *Tom Brown's Schooldays* in which the pious Arthur shames his schoolfellows by insisting upon saying his prayers – nods to Gene Wolfe's *Book of the New Sun* sequence (1980–1983), a work famously operating through wordplay, hint and allusion to oscillate on the boundaries of science fiction and fantasy.[20] Book Three of *Pyramids* is entitled 'The Book of the New Son'. We turn the pages to the text, and the next two words are, surely knowingly, '*the sun*' (P 155, 157).

One of the most thorough examinations of intertextuality in Pratchett is by Rzyman,[21] with many examples, not only from

Shakespeare and Lovecraft, but also from Kurt Vonnegut (25–26), T. S. Eliot (41–42), William Wordsworth (46) and the cartoonist Gary Larson (68–70). Whether this is all deliberate insertion of 'white knowledge' or simply the 'undigested information' of a very well-read author slipping into his text is not necessarily relevant, because Rzyman's particular issue is the difficulty this produces for the translator. How does the Polish translator cope, for example with the celebrated 'eldritch'? Options may include using an equivalent Polish archaism, or at least to use adjectives employed in Polish translations of Lovecraft. Neither of these options have consistently been followed, with the result that '[t]he Polish reader does not stand a snowball's chance in hell of seeing how Pratchett pays tribute to Lovecraft'.[22] But Rzyman does show how wordplay and allusion are the engine of story for Pratchett, and the shaping of story is both his technique and major preoccupation. Pratchett stirs his 'Cauldron of Story' by manipulating language and narrative.

LANGUAGE AND PUNS

Pratchett delights in language. When he puns, or invents a comic name, the wordplay *means* something. Vetinari, the Patrician of Ankh-Morpork, reflects the equally ruthless Medici family of the Italian Renaissance. Each name makes us think about rulers concerned with the health of the body politic, with the joke illuminated when, in *Feet of Clay*, a poisoned Vetinari is treated by the horse-doctor – or *veterinary* – Doughnut Jimmy. Agnes Nitt, important in *Lords and Ladies*, *Maskerade* and *Carpe Jugulum*, possibly reflects the seventeenth-century witch Agnes Nutter (herself based upon an historical *Alice* Nutter, executed 1612), whose 'prophecies' are part of the framework of Pratchett and Gaiman's *Good Omens*. Her alter ego Perdita is both the 'lost' romantic aspect of herself and a reference to the Princess/ Shepherdess of Shakespeare's *The Winter's Tale*. Perdita X. Dream is the acerbic, cool, gothically interesting, *thin* alternative to the teenager whose big hair and large body mark her out as the calm and capable eternal 'best friend'.

Humour often works by reversing linguistic expectations, especially those of cliché. If camels are famously 'ships of the desert', then to a desert culture unfamiliar with ships, the 'things like big rafts' must be 'camels of the sea' (*P* 197). Metaphors and other figures of speech become literalised or challenged. In keeping with the narrative personification which is a feature of Discworld and its characters, there are actual geographical locations for the Place Where The Sun Does Not Shine where we may be invited to stick something, or the Rock and the Hard Place between which many people find themselves. Metaphors themselves give up the ghost when confronted with characters like Archchancellor Ridcully, for whom using one as an explanation 'was like a red flag to a bu – was like putting something very annoying in front of someone who was annoyed by it' (*LL* 41). Statements are misunderstood or forensically unpicked to explore the truth beneath them. In *Hogfather*, Ridcully remarks that Hogswatch (Christmas) is 'not the time for silly arguments' only for his staff to point out that it is *exactly* the time when silly arguments, sulks, family feuds and inappropriate gift-giving are most prevalent (*H* 187). Language is twisted to reveal a point hidden in the pun: 'NO JUSTICE. JUST US', says Death (*RM* 231).

We expect to see Nanny Ogg being smutty. The reversal in *Carpe Jugulum*, when the prudish Magrat shocks the 'unshockable' Nanny with a sexual remark, reminds us that Magrat, as a married woman, is now 'qualified' to spar verbally with Nanny on sexual matters. This linguistic 'carnivalesque' links Pratchett to what the Russian literary theorist Mikhail Bakhtin called heteroglossia (*raznorechie*): the presence in a text of an actual multiplicity of texts, tones, dialects, relationships and references. Andrew M. Butler, in applying theories of humour to Pratchett's work, examines *Mort* as a novel in which we can plainly see the elements of inversion, scatological parody and insulting friendship which Bakhtin finds in the works of Rabelais.[23] Neither Mort, Death's apprentice, nor Ysabel, Death's adopted daughter, are entirely comfortable with the assumption that *of course* apprentices marry daughters. Ysabel tells Mort that she wouldn't marry him if he was the last man on the Disc, hurting his feelings even though he doesn't want to marry *her* either. They trade insults about each others' appearance, finally agreeing: 'Obviously we shouldn't get married, if only for the sake of the children' (*M* 100).

Pratchett creates more incongruity by using the language of one situation in the context of another. The assassin Teppic in *Pyramids* begins his examination by being ordered, in the language of a driving test to 'proceed' at his own pace 'obeying all signs and so forth' through a complicated route set with deadly traps (*P* 14). The rendition of the story of the Tsortean Wars told by the 'greatest storyteller in the history of the world' Copolymer (whose name comes from the chemical process of building complex arrangements of very large molecules from repeating subunits, and whose final syllable echoes the poet credited with exactly that literary technique) shows Pratchett reducing epic to chaotic rambling, only just retaining the 'units' of the story:

> Elenor, that was her name [...]. Anyway, there was this wooden horse and after they'd got in [...] Did I tell you about this horse? It was a horse. I'm pretty sure it was a horse [...] It was wossname's idea'. (*P* 189)
>
> [...]
>
> 'It's the way he remembers every tiny detail. Pin-sharp', murmured Ibid. (*P* 190)

STORY FRAGMENTS (THE THINGS WE KNOW)

Much of Pratchett's humour draws, like Copolymer's oral tradition, upon such fragments of half-understood and uncontextualised information surrounding art in a mass culture: how we recognise an allusion or quotation divorced from its origin. The foundations of *Wyrd Sisters* and *Maskerade* are the 'all we know' about Shakespeare and opera. Behind *Interesting Times* are the 'collection of ideas and cultural memes through which western popular culture sees China'.[24]

Wyrd Sisters begins with what 'everyone knows' from *Macbeth*. Magrat earnestly asks if Granny can tell someone is approaching by the pricking of her thumbs. The witches squabble about details of the 'poisoned entrails' to be thrown into the cauldron. A running joke of ever-increasing gruesomeness is the murderous Duke Felmet's attempts to remove bloodstains from his hand by washing, scrubbing and sandpapering. We know that in Shakespeare the obsessive hand-washer is actually *Lady* Macbeth. But we also know from 'On Fairy-stories' that story fragments become attached to more than one person, and the joke works better attached to the increasingly unstable Felmet.

Maskerade develops the 'witches' triad of Maiden, Mother, Crone. The Lancre witches are now missing the married, and therefore unqualified-as-Maiden Magrat, and much of the plot concerns how this lack is going to resolve itself. It also draws upon another set of 'white knowledge'. Nanny Ogg summarises what 'everybody knows' about opera:

> There's your heavy opera, where basically people sing foreign and it goes like 'Oh oh oh, I am dyin', oh, I am dyin', oh, oh, oh, that's what I'm doin'', and there's your light opera, where they sing in foreign and it basically goes 'Beer! Beer! Beer! Beer! I like to drink lots of beer!' (*Ma* 116)

And, of course, since the success of the 1986 Andrew Lloyd Weber musical, everyone knows that there *must* be a phantom of the opera.

Maskerade's plot is more sophisticated than earlier Pratchett. The essential joke about an Opera Ghost committing murders leads to a complex juggling of masks: personifying one of Pratchett's central themes, the struggle with self- or externally-imposed roles. Most of the characters, from the 'odd' janitor Walter Plinge to the famous singer Enrico Basilica, are, like Agnes/Perdita, essentially doubled: we even see Nanny Ogg's disreputable cat Greebo as Lord Gribeau accompanying Granny Weatherwax in her disguise as the immensely rich Lady Esmerelda. Agnes's beautiful singing voice leads to her being a voice double for the less talented but stunningly beautiful Christine. What this also leads to, of course, in the on-stage chaos when all the plot threads are being resolved, is the joke set up all along, when everyone turns to the buxom Agnes to bring the scene to its inevitable finish.

Interesting Times incorporates a range of Western stereotypes of Chinese cultures, from the ancient (the Great Wall, terracotta warriors) to the modern (an underground revolutionary movement agitating against the empire). There are references to foot-binding, food (a reference to 'chow', the slang term for food, which also hints that it is the name of a breed of dog) and the importance of calligraphy and poetry in obtaining a career in the Civil Service. There are echoes of Sun Tzu's *Art of War* and blue-and-white willow pattern ceramics. If *Maskerade* essentially plays upon what 'everyone knows' about opera – mannered singing, phantom, and the physique of divas – *Interesting Times* throws up a multitude of stereotypes and exaggerations, not only from Chinese history but from other East Asian cultures. Origami, sumo wrestlers and Noh theatre are also referenced. Rincewind being Rincewind, there are jokes about his cowardice, and how his inability to master the very different language results in him saying the most incongruous things in moments of stress. Hajdu's essay on Pratchett's use of Chinese features in the novel, which distort historical and cultural backgrounds as much as they reflect them, argues that they 'help create a world in which a fascinating and meaningful story can evolve'.[25] But while contrasts between the rigid social dynamics of the Empire and the anarchic individualism of Anhk-Morpork provide interesting and effective comedy, it might be argued that the music-hall humour of the stereotypes (behind it all, one feels the presence of Gilbert and Sullivan's 1885 comic opera *The Mikado*) cosies the social critique, leaving 'a general scepticism about the possibility of perfect social arrangements or even the viability of rapid changes'.[26]

As well as quotations, catchphrases and factoids, there are also what in folklore analysis might be called the motifs, but in this context might be called the genre expectations: what Farah Mendlesohn in *Rhetorics of Fantasy* calls 'that common bible of expectations'.[27] We expect, for instance, in fantasy, to come across the 'rightful King' story: central to *The Lord of the Rings* and woven by Pratchett skilfully into *Wyrd Sisters*, developing in *Guards! Guards!* from Brother Watchtower's solemn assurance that rightful heirs happen all the time – 'They go lurking around in the distant wildernesses for ages, handing down the secret sword and birthmark and so forth from generation to generation' (*GG* 14) – to Carrot's sword which is nameless, unmagical, lacking any sense of destiny about it, and, therefore 'practically unique' (*GG* 23). This thread continues in *Men at Arms* and is left deliberately unresolved despite evidence pointing to the dwarf-adopted Carrot as rightful king of Ankh-Morpork. We also find, in a certain type of 'hard-boiled' crime fiction, something natural in a cop's drunken reflection about the city being like a woman who lets you fall in love with her then kicks you in the teeth and *then* catches you off balance so that you can never let her go. Edward James identifies in the Night Watch series echoes of Ed McBain and Raymond Chandler, as well as the 1948 film *The Naked City*, and a phrase ('just the facts, ma'am') from the 1950s American cop show *Dragnet* familiar to many who have never seen the programme (*GOL* 196–197). He also reminds us that Carrot belongs to another tradition, that of the cheery British bobby whose touchstone is probably the long-running BBC TV series *Dixon of Dock Green* (1955–1976).[28] Carrot quotes several catchphrases from the programme (in Dwarfish).

Pratchett, though, does not just jokingly nod to our expectations of genre by quoting catchphrases. He explores and develops. Just as Lady Macbeth's lines hold more dramatic impact in *Wyrd Sisters* when uttered by the Macbeth-analogue Felmet, Vimes's monologue, though 'almost identical'[29] to the opening of McBain's *The Mugger* (1956),[30] is reworked to make it more what the laws of story demand. McBain actually wrote: 'The city could be nothing but a woman' not from a drunken cop but through the viewpoint of his *villain*.[31] Pratchett gives us such passages not how we would read them, were we to be so pedantic as to check the original, but how we *remember* them, entangling us once again with 'white knowledge'. When these story fragments weave together, something more than joke or satire takes place.

A major source of both anxiety and humour is how humans tend to behave like characters in stories. Pratchett finds his deepest vein of humour (and his darkest morality tales) in showing how stereotypical or formulaic stories become excuses to impose roles on others. Everybody knows from folklore that old women who live alone in woods are witches, just as everybody knows, from reading Tolkien, that orcs and goblins are evil. *Witches Abroad* opens with a meditation upon stories. Stories are not shaped by people: quite the reverse. Stories exist independently from people.

NARRATIVE CAUSALITY

Parodying our need for an explanation that looks scientific, Pratchett calls this process 'narrative causality'. Story 'takes a shape' (*WA* 8), imposing patterns on history and moulding events. Unlike our cause-and-effect universe, Discworld operates through narrative and personification, with dragons breathing fire 'because everyone knows that's what dragons *do*'.[32] Death is skeletal and carries a scythe. We know this from countless medieval images. Million-to-one chances *always* succeed in popular fiction, although the odds might have to be adjusted so that they are *exactly* a million to one (*GG* 240–241). In Discworld, something like the medieval doctrine of correspondences (plants, for instance, healing body parts they resemble) holds sway, forcing plot and character in the story to act according to type. *If*, for instance, stone circles such as Stonehenge were some form of calendar-fixing computing devices, so the Druids operating them in *The Light Fantastic must* talk like computer nerds.

Part of *Witches Abroad* is its own games with the 'parasitical' nature of story. In the age-old 'three witches' trope of Crone–Mother–Maiden, Nanny Ogg is cheerfully happy in her role as 'disgusting old baggage'. Magrat is the 'wet hen' dissatisfied with being picked on but unable (so far) to 'find herself' until she unexpectedly inherits her position as Fairy Godmother. Granny herself is already actively fighting against acting according to story. Both here, and in subsequent witches novels such as *Carpe Jugulum*, Granny struggles against becoming Black Aliss, the wicked witch from the European tradition with the gingerbread cottage and sinister oven. Granny's elder sister Lily is the 'bad' Fairy Godmother who has turned the city of Genua into a stereotypical fairy-story realm or, as Kevin Paul Smith tells us, a Baudrillardian hyperreality or 'third order simulation' reminiscent of Disneyland.[33] Pratchett even uses the term Magic Kingdom (a well-known theme park operated by the Disney Corporation) in a passage describing Lily's ambition. In their domestic struggle of roles, Granny is forced to be 'the good one' while Lily, convinced *she* knows best, is determined to *make* people act according to narrative. In Lily's Genua a toymaker is tortured for the crime of failing to whistle and tell stories to children. Part of the chilly undertone to the Red Riding Hood parody which forms a digression on the way to Genua is that the characters have *only* acted like stereotypes. The woodcutters have only seen the wolf (and '[y]ou don't talk to *wolves*'). The mad old woman is obviously a witch because she lives alone in the wood, has a hook nose and no teeth, and mutters to herself. Granny's response to this is to remind the woodcutter of *choice*:

'You could have seen to the old woman', she said quietly. 'You could have talked to the wolf. But you didn't, right?' (*WA* 116)

Later, the confrontation between Granny and Mrs Gogol focuses on the balance within Granny of light and dark.

'But she might do something—dreadful'.

'Good. She's always wanted to', said Nanny. (*WA* 233)

After Lily left home, says Granny, '*I* had to be the good one. You had all the fun'. 'But I... I... I'm the good one', Lily responds: 'I can't lose. I'm the godmother. You're the wicked witch' (*WA* 243).

What is the difference? Karen Sayer suggests that Lily cannot distinguish between her *self* and her *image*. Neither sister can truly be said to have authored her own life: but Granny *knows* this, and is determined to fight 'storying' tendencies. When Death traps them both inside the mirror, it is Granny who can identify her real self:

Fascinated by her stories and her mirrors [Lily] lives in the world of what Lacan has called the Imaginary – the world a child lives in before it recognises that it is an individual separate and distinct from its mother. Granny, who always knows who she is, belongs to the world of the 'I', or what psychologists call the Symbolic Order. She can assert herself as a distinct and separate subjectivity, or person, different from other people.[34]

But moral choice trumps character and role. As Granny says to Lily: 'You shouldn't treat people like they was *characters*, like they was *things*' (*WA* 238).

THE STRUGGLE WITH STORY

Granny, however, is not the only character to struggle against narrative causality or to question the function of story. The Crone–Mother–Maiden triptych blurs in interesting ways. In *Carpe Jugulum*, Nanny Ogg is faced with the possibility of becoming the Crone and doesn't like it. Magrat is, by *Maskerade*, no longer 'Maiden' and by *Carpe Jugulum*, her 'replacement' Agnes is cloaking her sexual desire for the preacher Mightily Oats by quibbling about the meaning of 'Maiden': 'A technical term for the junior member of a trio of witches' (*CJ* 167). Granny herself, as Nanny Ogg reveals to Archchancellor Mustrum Ridcully in *Lords and Ladies*, has always been two of the three: 'she's qualified, ain't she? When it comes to unicorn taming' (*LL* 271). Magrat, overcoming her 'wet hen' role by donning the armour of warrior-queen Ynci to fight the elves is, unknowingly, channelling an entirely fictional personality. Story works in strange ways, as we find with Watch commander Sam Vimes, increasingly and uneasily aware that his progression up Ankh-Morpork's social ladder is at odds with his origin in the Shades and his character as cynical anti-authoritarian idealist. In *Night Watch*, Vimes is entangled with the historical story of Ankh-Morpork, which is also his own. Pursuing the murderer Carcer through time he must assume the identity of the Watchman who mentored his younger self, and observe the national story and his own personal narrative unfolding, aware that there is no guarantee that either will unfold in the same way. Carcer taunts Vimes because he *knows* that a policeman's badge ensures that he will play 'by the book'. Vimes removes the badge to allow the confrontation full play and give the Beast full rein. But Vimes knows that face to face with the Beast within him, without the protection of the narrative causality of the policeman who must obey the rules, he must avoid giving in to his instincts: 'If you did, Carcer won' (*NW* 358).

When Malicia and Keith, in *Amazing Maurice*, are tied up by the Rat-Catchers, Malicia goes through all the possibilities of escape that would exist if Keith was a story-book hero with a hidden knife or matches, or secret powers. Unfortunately, he isn't. Malicia is chided for believing that real life *isn't* just a story. But although when she first appears in the novel she is gently mocked for her constant fantasising, she has a point: 'If you don't turn your life into a story, you just become a part of someone else's story'. If your story doesn't work, 'You keep changing it until you find one that does' (*AM* 148).

Glenda and Juliet in *Unseen Academicals* perhaps echo too closely the similar relationship between 'competent' and 'glamorous' women we found in Agnes and Christine in *Maskerade*. But Glenda learns sooner than Agnes that it is wrong for her to live her empty-headed friend's life for her. *Unseen Academicals*, like *Maskerade* and many later Pratchett novels, oscillates between farce and relentless probing at the nature of the narratives shaping our lives. In this case, the need for Unseen University to field a football team to secure its finances under the terms of an endowment leads to typical 'all we know about football' jokes. The story of Mr Nutt, apparently a goblin sent from Überwald (the wilder, less organised mirror-image of Ankh-Morpork) to work at the university, allows Pratchett to look more seriously at social tensions, although each thread offers more engagement with narrative causality. The symbolism of the crabs keeping each other back in the crab bucket (*UA* 218) shows how both Glenda and Juliet are restrained by expectations of class and gender. The contrast between the articulate Mr Nutt and his friend Trev offers scope for double-edged humour. Nutt is educated by having the run of his mentor Ladyship's library in Überwald. Trev, son of football star Dave Likely, is educated in the Shove, the football crowd. Both are in their own crab bucket; Nutt obeying embedded instructions to fit in, not to stand out from the crowd, to stay safe and not be threatening, and Trev held back by both his role as a 'likely lad' in football-culture and his promise to his mother not to risk his life in the game after his father's death.

In the struggle with story, it all depends upon how we *tell* the story. Before the football match, reluctant hero Trev was 'Dave Likely's son'. *After* it, 'they said Dave Likely was your father' (*UA* 386). The focus has changed. And Nutt, too, grows to taking control over his own story, accepting his origins as an Orc and understanding that history is not the same as *his story*. Some of the truth of Nutt's origins are 'behind the door' in his head, and while this leads to jokes about psychoanalysis – the accent; the Freudian urge to smoke a cigar – what we are shown in Nutt's mind is yet another text: a book. 'The book was called *ORC*' (*UA* 266). It is the narrative of this book (of course indebted to Tolkien's portrayal of Orcs as irredeemably mindless evil creatures) which Nutt realises can be changed. We are, it seems, hiding from ourselves what we do not want to hear (*UA* 272). One of these hidden narratives is that the story of the creation of the Orcs by an Evil Empire is a convenient 'truth' that allows human responsibility to be slid aside and overlooked. In *Unseen Academicals*, personal and collective agency are woven together to stress responsibility. It is a carefully constructed recipe, to the point where Pratchett plays with the concept of 'happy endings', one of which includes the just desserts of sociopathic hooligan Andy Shank served up by a character without the inner 'niceness' of Trev or Glenda. It is easy to read Pratchett's jokes about narrative causality and the forcing of individuals into 'storied' roles as cosy games with language and popular culture. It is particularly tempting to do so because his novels are playful fantasies, even though the role of fantasy, as he says, is to 'take something so familiar that we no longer see it' and allow readers to look at it anew.[35] But if his novels have ever been cosy, by *Unseen Academicals* the relationship between *story* and *storied* is much more complicated.

The Colour of Magic shows gods playing games with humans as pawns. In later novels, this is left to the politicians. Vetinari manipulates and changes the 'stories' of Moist von Lipwig, making him responsible for developing Ankh-Morpork by modernising the postal and financial systems, and of Sam Vimes. Vimes is a pawn, but an increasingly active one (as policeman, as concerned with the safety of the 'polis' as any politician), increasingly capable of standing his ground when his own moral compass is activated. Both the football and the Orc arcs of *Unseen Academicals* are paid close attention to by Vetinari and Margolotta (Ladyship) because in their different ways they affect the internal and external relationships of their realms. The individual lives of Trev, Glenda, Juliet, even Nutt, and the minor characters are subordinate to the Great Power diplomatic relations going on above and around them. *Unseen Academicals* ends, though, with Nutt revising the laws of football with Vetinari on equal terms, and reminding Margolotta that 'It's Mister Nutt, if you please' (*UA* 393). If victory over narrative causality cannot be fully achieved, it is nonetheless possible to allow oneself not to be defeated.

6

Fantasy or Science Fiction?

When Jack Cohen and Ian Stewart approached Pratchett with the idea for *The Science of Discworld*, the 'fatal flaw in the plan' was that '[t]here is *no* science in Discworld'.[1] The rules of Discworld are the rules of fantasy and narrative causality – dragons breathing fire because dragons in stories *do*. The 'cauldron of story' Pratchett draws from is that of fantasy and magic. However, although his early interest in science and astronomy was not followed through academically because of a deficiency in mathematics, Pratchett remained fascinated by science, technology and gadgetry. As a writer who began with science fiction, he employed the language of sf throughout his fiction. In the early Discworld novels he playfully highlighted elements undermining scientific certainty, compared to which 'a large turtle with a world on its back is practically mundane' (*WA* 8). These include such complications as chaos theory and the phenomenon of sensitive dependence on initial conditions leading to the so-called 'butterfly effect' in which (allegedly) a butterfly flapping its wings in one part of the world results in a hurricane elsewhere. The Quantum Weather Butterfly is featured in *Interesting Times*, and hinted at as 'that bloody butterfly whose flapping wings cause all these storms we've been having lately' in *Witches Abroad* (*WA* 7). Through the heated and often surreal disputes among the Unseen University faculty, we explore the nature of science (and magic) as devices for understanding the world.

Repeated throughout is the joke about the way the word 'quantum' constantly comes to the lips of Ponder Stibbons when he is trying to explain something. The language of science is increasingly used for the 'magic' elements. Stibbons's explanation, in *Interesting Times*, of how Rincewind can be transported to the Counterweight Continent uses scientific terms like 'energy absorption and attention to relative velocities' (*IT* 19), the parameters of which are worked out by Hex, the University's magical equivalent of a supercomputer.

The Science of Discworld and its succeeding volumes examines the difference between the operating systems of Discworld and our own Roundworld, and finds them not as dissimilar as they might appear. In fact, our universe is operated by magic for (to use a phrase often used by Stewart and Cohen) a given value of 'magic'. We in Roundworld spend much of our time compensating for its lack of narrativium and anthropomorphic personification by constructing stories about how our world works. We are not *homo sapiens* (Wise Human) but *pan narrans*, the Storytelling Chimpanzee, painting stories upon the universe – stories called, variously, Religion, Mythology and Science. This does not mean that Stewart and Cohen are not committed to the story of science as an explanation of the universe, but that much of science itself is 'storied' – either because it is easy to construct narratives ('This is the story of human evolution') or because we need simplified versions in order to help us progress to more complex truths. The technology of the motor car, the chemistry of the chlorophyll reaction, how a TV set works – all these are (as far as most of us are concerned) 'magical'. The Lies-to-Children, by which we explain natural phenomena like 'why is the sky blue' are only 'true' for a given value of 'truth'. The 'story of science' is constructed in our world by means of our shared cultural memes. This is not to say that, for example, the path of the earth around the sun is something socially constructed, but that we smooth out the complicated bits. We know the *Earth* is turning, but we *see* sun*rises* and sun*sets*.

Melanie Keene's *Science in Wonderland* (2015) explored how so many Victorian writers for children turned to the fairy tale to 'explain' scientific discoveries and theories. The fairy-tale perspectives given by Charles Kingsley's *The Water Babies* (1863) or Arabella Buckley's *The Fairyland of Science* (1879) helped to confront the paradigm shifts thrown to geology and natural history by Lyell and Darwin, which certainly needed convenient and attractive 'lies-to-children' to be explained. But the Science of Discworld series is neither a sugar-coated attempt to explain science to fantasy fans, nor the kind of fannish game which has fun with 'explaining'

Discworld with modern scientific vocabulary. Instead, we are taken through the presentation of Discworld as 'thought-experiment' into examinations of how 'stories of science' are constructed and how science interrogates itself.

The encounter in *The Last Continent* with the God of Evolution who, like Charles Darwin, has a fondness for beetles, is one of Pratchett's most extended parodies of science and the scientific method. Evolution on the Discworld is a matter of direct intervention by a god – a god who, in typical Discworld fashion, thinks that wheeled elephants are an interesting idea. The idea of hands-on involvement tempts Ponder Stibbons, especially as he can see where the god might be going wrong in some of his designs. The god has never quite understood, for instance, that elephants can be made by *other elephants*, which leads the easily embarrassed Stibbons towards a discussion of the role of sex from which he is rescued by Mrs Whitlow, the University housekeeper who is the subject of many furtive fantasies in the mind of the Senior Wrangler. Ponder hopes that his work with the god on the big project, designing a life-form resourceful and adaptable enough to survive in almost any circumstances and conditions, will result in a better-designed human, but the god has already designed what fits the bill: a cockroach. There is, of course, no fundamental reason to assume that the purpose of evolution is to progress towards humanity as the highest goal. Stewart and Cohen extend this discussion in *Darwin's Watch*, which dramatises the religious and scientific interpretations of evolution as understood in William Paley's *Natural Theology* (1802) and Darwin's *On The Origin of Species* (1859). Paley's Watchmaker argument – that the discovery of a complicated mechanism such as a watch implies the existence of a watch*maker*, and that this can also be the case for a complicated biological structure such as the eye – was countered by Darwin's hypothesis of natural selection: a process of constant infinitesimal change as organisms adapt to the contexts of their environment, itself in a constant process of change. In the context of Victorian ideas, the relationship of Darwinist natural selection to theism exists in a vast phase-space of possibilities. It is not so much that Darwinism is true and Paley's Watchmaker analogy was false, but that each is an explanation within the context of a range of other beliefs about how the universe works.

TECHNOLOGY

Of all the Discworld books, the Changes series, from *The Truth* to *Raising Steam*, is closer to science fiction if sf is assumed to be about knowledge and understanding the world. In *Raising Steam*, Pratchett is at his most explicitly emphatic that he is writing about change. Technological invention is frequently satirised through visionaries like Leonard of Quirm whose fertile imagination and childlike naivety make him one of the most dangerous men on Discworld, and the surreally crazy inventions of B. S. (Bloody Stupid) Johnson, credited in *Going Postal* for a wheel in which *pi* (the ratio of its circumference to its diameter) is exactly 3 rather than the 'untidy' 3.14159 and in *Men at Arms* for a maze so small people get lost looking for it (*GP* 146; *MAA* 58). The sketches of Leonardo da Vinci are the bases of the devices of Leonard of Quirm, the designer of the advanced weapon (the 'gonne') foolishly kept by the Assassins in *Men at Arms*. Leonard (whose submarine in *Jingo* is the basis of an extended comic routine) is, because of the potential danger of his inventions, imprisoned by Vetinari, but still allowed to create his models (the 'flapping-wing-flying-device', and the 'spinning-up-into-the-air machine') and dream dreams of how the freedom of the air would bring an end to war.

The 'gonne' is returned to hiding, thanks to the understanding between Carrot himself, whose goodness prevents him from succumbing to the new kind of power implied by such a weapon, and Vetinari. However, in later Discworld novels we see developments which, despite fantasy trappings, are much more akin to those science fiction novels in which conceptual breakthroughs or new technologies ensure that the world is never the same again. In *The Truth*, for example, we have something which changes the relationship between rulers and ruled: the invention of moveable type and printing, which leads to Ankh-Morpork's first newspaper.

The novel plays with a figure of speech: the rumour spreading around the city is that '[t]he dwarfs can turn lead into gold' (*TT* 9). This transmutation, of course, is the goal of medieval (and Discworld) alchemists and implies fantasy or magic. What happens is a more figurative relationship between lead type and money: the lucrative partnership between William de Worde, first seen engraving monthly news reports to the rulers of other cities, and the dwarf entrepreneur Gunilla Goodmountain (Gutenberg). What results is an additional twist to the uneasy alliance between politician Vetinari and policeman Vimes as 'men of the city' as a third force (the Press) results from the establishment of a newspaper whose slogan is variously (and equally validly) 'the truth shall make ye free' or (thanks to a series of typographical errors) 'the truth shall make ye fret'.

From *Going Postal*, life within and around Ankh-Morpork is changed by the adoption of the 'clacks', the semaphore system revolutionising communication between the cities of the Discworld. Pratchett adopts elements of the electrical telegraph (and the modern Internet) to emphasise the way technology, especially communications technology, affects society, inspiring and speeding up social change. *Going Postal* shifts the tone of Discworld from post-medieval to a recognisable satire on modern corporate capitalism as we learn that the clacks has become a cash-cow for unscrupulous developers. The Smoking Gnu, the trio of former clacks workers whose signalling expertise steers Moist von Lipwig and Adora Belle Dearheart to victory in their contest with Reacher Gilt, are recognisably derived from hacker teams such as the Lone Gunmen from *The X-Files*. Pratchett carefully makes the clacks consistent as technology (it does not work by magic). In *Making Money*, von Lipwig modernises yet another moribund institution, the Bank. In *Raising Steam*, the Discworld discovers the delights of the locomotive thanks to the ingenuity of Dick Simnel, who persuades the entrepreneur Harry King to back his concept for harnessing the power of steam. Here, Pratchett is at his most explicitly emphatic that he is writing about the concept of change: 'the future is coming down the track fast. And who knows what is going to arrive next?' (*RS* 136). But this is change which develops not from the earlier pseudo-medieval fantasy-world basis of Discworld, but from a Discworld already affected by the technologies and social structures in previous novels, flavoured by stereotypes we know: Simnel's northern (British) working-class accent and the promotion of 'Sir' Harry King to the title of 'Baron', recalling the term 'robber baron' coined in the late nineteenth century to describe exploitative and unscrupulous American businessmen. Vetinari keeps his position by means of his ability to manage change through roguish manipulators such as Moist von Lipwig and geniuses such as Simnel – practical men rather than theoretical visionaries like Leonard of Quirm – but people with the ability to create change. Above all, *Raising Steam*, with its emphasis upon the process of change, also suggests that change depends upon context, for as Charles Fort noted: 'A social growth cannot find out the use of steam engines, until comes steam-engine-time'.[2] *Raising Steam* derives from that remark, repeated several times by Vetinari to Lady Margolotta:

> 'Madam, only a fool would try to stop the progress of the multitude. Vox populi, vox deorum, carefully shepherded by a thoughtful prince, of course. And so I take the view that when it's steam engine time steam engines will come' (*RS* 23)

and by Lu-Tze the History Monk to Mustrum Ridcully:

> 'But even the Abbot is disturbed about the arrival of steam engines when it isn't steam-engine-time'. (*RS* 112)

SOCIETY AND CHANGE

There is not, of course, only technological and social innovation to spark change. Ankh-Morpork, whose national anthem proclaims 'We Can Rule You Wholesale' (*BOTS* 268–270), becomes revealed as an increasingly cosmopolitan city as Pratchett uses the traditional fantasy cast of different species to explore pressures of city life and racial tensions. Vetinari's encouragement of 'diversity' within the Watch – making the sometimes-reluctant Vimes recruit Dwarfs, Trolls, Werewolves, Vampires, Gnomes – allows these tensions to be observed. Angua, for instance, is concerned that her werewolf nature will affect her relationship with Carrot, who, before he has discovered her identity, has confessed to wishing that the 'undead' would 'go back to where they came from' (*MAA* 78). There are tensions between her and the Dwarf Cheery Littlebottom (*Feet of Clay*), and the new Vampire recruit 'Sally' (*Thud!*). Ankh-Morpork is, to the surprise of Vimes when told this in *The Fifth Elephant*, the biggest Dwarf city outside Überwald; and the factional conflicts of Dwarf Society, embodied by the 'deep-downers' or 'grags' who are the guardians of traditional dwarf lore, are brought into the city. In *Thud!*, we are told that both troll and dwarf population in Ankh-Morpork expanded under Vetinari, and the tension between dwarfs and trolls, traditional enemies since the Battle of Koom Valley, leads to riots. In the early novels, this rivalry/enmity is there for largely comic effect. By *Thud!*, Pratchett is showing us the roots of virtually any national hatred in passages which, with minor changes of vocabulary, could describe the Real world:

> Where any dwarf fought any troll, there was Koom Valley. Even if it was a punch-up in a pub, it was Koom Valley. It was part of the mythology of both races. (*Th* 31)

Vimes is instrumental in the peace brokered between Dwarfs and Trolls, a peace that continues to be full of tension but is not the all-out war that is threatened in *Thud!*.

This process of exploring and expanding upon the cultural environments within his novels is perhaps another area in which Pratchett's work is more akin to science fiction than to fantasy. This begins, as much of Pratchett's development does, with humour. The fact that the six-foot tall Carrot is culturally a dwarf is simply comic in the early novels – maybe, as he remarks in *Guards! Guards!*, he is just tall for his height – as are many aspects of the dwarfs themselves, such as belligerence, fondness for 'quaffing' (often missing your mouth altogether when you drink), singing songs which are simply the repetition of the word 'gold', and their reticence about gender, which is 'more or less optional' (*GG* 26) – a phrase packed full of ironic implications teased out in later novels. As the sequence progresses, Pratchett begins to eschew stereotype and slapstick, and the dwarfs become part of a more subtle and nuanced form of satire. Somewhat easy jokes about height (the Campaign for Equal Heights defending dwarf rights to be equal citizens) gives way to Vimes's understanding that he actually knows very little about dwarf society, which is just as complicated – and even more ridden with factions and feuds – as the human one he knows so well. The 'deep-downers', distrusting those surface-dwellers, are in part a satire of fundamentalists of all sorts (down to the pun inherent in 'fundamental') but give political dimensions to the narrative. The reticence about gender starts with a comic shift – with Pratchett gradually revealing that new recruit Cheery Littlebottom is female and wants to embrace femininity – but continues with further and more politically charged revelations in *Raising Steam.*

Pratchett's Dwarfs draw upon a long literary/folklorist tradition of being depicted as miners, smiths and technologists. The dwarfs Granny takes her broomstick to in *Equal Rites* are the typical car repairers who blame high prices upon the technology: 'it's hard to get the bristles these days' (*ER* 102). By *The Truth*, Gunilla Goodmountain is operating a printing press and there is no sense that magic is involved. By *Thud!*, the Dwarfs have weapons (actually, tools) that can fire flame, and are in possession of power-supplying 'Devices' such as the perpetual-motion mechanism Carrot shows Vetinari, which powers one of the biggest mines in Überwald: 'We don't know how they're made, they're very rare, but the other three I've heard of have not stopped working for hundreds of years. They don't use fuel, they don't need anything' (*Th* 140).

At this point, we are in the territory described by Arthur C. Clarke's Third Law: 'Any sufficiently advanced technology is indistinguishable from magic'.[3] In *Thud!* we learn that Vetinari has pondered upon the implications of this 'advanced technology' for Ankh-Morpork, and is planning an 'Undertaking' to construct roads and drains under the city. But the concerns of *Snuff* are more political than technological, and the next Discworld novel is *Raising Steam*, in which essentially nineteenth-century steam-powered locomotives are favoured over the Devices. If there were any attempts develop Discworld in a more overtly science-fictional way, perhaps recalling the proto-Discworld of *Strata*, they are victims of the steamroller to which, in accordance with his wishes, Pratchett's family and assistant consigned his computer hard drives containing drafts and story ideas.

The acceptance of goblins, a species treated as 'vermin' and forced to the edges, is the subject of *Snuff*. The crimes Vimes solves in his enforced holiday in the Ramkin country mansion begin with the murder of a young goblin woman, which draws him into investigating a network of slavery. *Snuff* is one of Pratchett's grimmest novels, but in some way his most problematic, as noted above. This is certainly so in the way the individual murderer is brought to justice while the young aristocrat behind the slavery/smuggling ring is allowed to flee the county because such 'stratagems and unseen expedients' (*Sn* 373) are part of Vetinari's overall Plan. Perhaps more sentimental is the way popular acceptance of the goblins as sentient feeling beings is brought about by the wonderful singing of Tears of the Mushroom rather than by physical or moral persuasion. Pratchett shows the economic face of Ankh-Morpork when Carrot and Angua interview Billy Slick, a goblin working for the entrepreneur Harry King who 'pay[s] them half what I pay humans and I reckon they do twice as much work, and do it better' (*S* 228). Billy lives willingly in the world of King (who as a dealer in waste products of all kinds has no illusions about how far he is accepted by Ankh-Morpork society), rejecting his goblin name (Of the Wind Regretfully Blown) because: 'This is modern times right? [...] Why the fruckle should anyone be proud of being a goblin?' (*S* 231), causing Angua (a werewolf whose own background was revealed in *The Fifth Elephant*) to consider the implications of Vetinari's 'grand design':

> 'and so one at a time we all become human – human werewolves, human trolls [...] the melting pot melts in once direction only, and so we make progress'. (*S* 230–231)

By *Raising Steam*, the goblins are skilled workers in the clacks, and making significant amounts of money by selling their sacred 'unggue pots' as souvenirs.

THE IMPORTANCE OF KNOWLEDGE

Throughout the Discworld series, Pratchett's attitude to book-learning is at first ambiguous. Perhaps in keeping with his background as a working-class journalist without a theory-based university background, we see a dismissive attitude to education drawn from books rather than experience, but as an autodidact whose education came from libraries, Pratchett at the same time argues the value of books. Characters like Nijel the Destroyer, learning how to be a barbarian hero from a manual, are figures of fun, while Pratchett's ambivalent attitude to being found 'guilty of literature' by literary critics is shown in the 'piles of small slim volumes of literary criticism' left behind by the 'critters [...] grazing on the contents of the choicer books' (*GG* 173). In fact, Nijel may be mocked, but *Sourcery*'s villain is Coin, who orders the destruction of a library of 90,000 volumes. There is a kind of resolution in *Small Gods*. Brutha, memorising the Ephebean library, saves knowledge uncontaminated by its pretensions as he cannot actually read. In *Truckers*, Masklin begins the nomes' exodus from the Store by insisting that everyone who wants (including women) is taught to read: 'Anything we want to do, there's a book that tells us how!' (*T* 113). Both stances – satire and more considered justification – operate in *Carpe Jugulum*, where Verence, kindly and well-meaning, but ineffectual, tries to teach himself 'kinging' out of books. Trying to do the right thing, Verence only goes as far as what is in the books, never thinking beyond them, parroting political clichés to Nanny Ogg and, under the belief that he is opening up his country to the wider world, brings about near-disaster by inviting vampires into the realm.

Mightily Oats, following the Omnian religion revised and reformed by Brutha, has a passion for knowledge which causes problems with his faith. Years of study in his country's new libraries shows him that sacred texts contradict each other and reflect other texts which aren't sacred. Brought up to believe that the Book of Om is Holy Writ, Oats nevertheless sacrifices it to keep Granny Weatherwax alive. Both Verence and Mightily Oats are similar characters; naïve and desperately well-meaning. It is Oats, however, who shows the more mature attitude that knowledge is a process, not mere learning of facts. Although Nijel and Verence read books instead of learning, and Mrs Earwig in the Tiffany Aching books even *writes* books obfuscating the truth about witchcraft, much more dangerous is the vacuum in the minds of the semi-literate Fred Colon, educated at 'the School of My Dad Always Said', and the 'College of It Stands to Reason' (*J* 28), and Mr Windling and his fellow-lodgers in *The Truth*, uncritically absorbing stories about elvish abductions.

Libraries, as repositories of knowledge, and books, as ways in which knowledge is propagated, are therefore vital. L-Space, in *Guards! Guards!* and elsewhere, is the phase-space which links all library catalogues and books together. In 'real' library systems, this linkage is only virtual, the metaphysical / metaphorical connection of linking threads between areas of knowledge which, in traditional libraries was operated by major classification schemes such as the Dewey Decimal or Library of Congress systems. While for most users the linkage is operated now by the World Wide Web, allowing internet users to search almost ad infinitum, the concept remains the same. L-Space embodies the very spirit of librarianship. Pratchett's 'conceit' – it is far too carefully constructed to be a simple 'joke' – is built around one of the few scientific equations to have become part of popular culture: $E=mc2$, the relationship between energy and mass (energy equals mass times the speed of light squared). We simply literalise the metaphor. 'Knowledge is power' is a phrase attributed to Francis Bacon in his *Meditationes Sacrae* (1597): *'ipsa scientia potestas est'*. By exploiting the double-meaning of the word 'power', Pratchett creates one of the greatest defences of libraries and librarians.

'[E]ven big collections of ordinary books distort space [...] The relevant equation is: knowledge=power=energy=matter=mass' (GG 8). Collections of books warp space and time, perhaps because a book itself is an exercise in warping space and time. Reading Tolstoy's *War and Peace*, for instance, in some ways brings us to nineteenth-century Russia, just as Olaf Stapledon's *Last and First Men* takes us millions of years into the future. Books are written under the influence of, even against, other books. Collections of books are a tangled mass of wormholes (or 'bookwormholes') linking the space-time continuum.

Discworld reminds us, though, that books can be dangerous. A book stolen from Unseen University Library in *Guards! Guards!* almost brings disaster upon Ankh-Morpork. If a little knowledge is a dangerous thing, then an entire library full of it is perilous. Jokes about dangerous magical grimoires remind us that the most fearsome threat to totalitarian regimes of all kinds is a 'subversive' book.

7

Morality and Ethics

In his introduction to the non-fiction collection *A Slip of the Keyboard*, Neil Gaiman wrote of 'Terry's underlying sense of what is fair and what is not' and his rage 'against so many things: stupidity, injustice, human foolishness and shortsightedness' (*ASOTK* n.p.). Like many humourists, Pratchett took his task as a writer of social commentary seriously, though never solemnly or patronizingly. He exposed the comic absurdity of humanity's search for moral absolutes and excuses for moral failure, but the absurdity is never nihilistic. The lens through which comedy is focused is a Swiftian exasperation with human folly and a Dickensian relish of the moral complications that that folly leads to. 'No-one ever thinks of themselves as one of Them. We're always one of Us. It's Them that do the bad things' (*J* 138).

Occasionally, Pratchett publicly expressed views which might be called political, but with a small 'p'. After his diagnosis with posterior cortical atrophy, he became a voice for the treatment of Alzheimer's disease and assisted dying, writing such pieces as the one reprinted in *A Slip of the Keyboard* as 'The NHS is Seriously Injured'. His fiction, as it developed, certainly contained as much rage as comedy. But if Pratchett *was*, in the end, 'guilty of literature' it is hard to argue that he was guilty of partisan politics. Discworld is not a meticulously planned universe. Characters change as new jokes, new situations in which their quirks may be highlighted, come to mind. While his views on religion might, throughout his work, show up as reasonably consistent, other areas are more problematic. John Newsinger's criticism of what he sees as the underlying defence of 'the maintenance of social order' in the Discworld sequence pointed to *Night Watch* as 'probably Pratchett's greatest joke ever: a revolution that is actually carried out by the police! [...] None of this left-wing socialism rubbish in Ankh-Morpork!'.[1] Certainly underlying the series *is* the problem of maintaining social order, where the carnivalesque inversion of Ankh-Morpork's 'normality' has to be corrected, but in an essay in Breton's *Power and Society in Terry Pratchett's Discworld*, Helena Esser argues that in *Night Watch* Pratchett is engaging in a more subtle interrogation of power structures in the face of injustice and corruption, and that Vimes is perfectly sincere in his 'rejection of top-down policing'.[2]

Jokes about Dwarf and Troll 'activism' (the Campaign For Equal Heights; the Silicon Anti-Defamation League) and the need to recruit 'minorities' into the Watch may be interpreted as swipes at that old chestnut of the Right, political correctness. Perhaps they were; but they never were *only* that, and Pratchett's most uncomfortable jokes are more pointed reminders of behaviour that encompass Left and Right: Tomjon's unthinking assumption in *Wyrd Sisters* that he can address a dwarf with a term used as a slur because they are friends, the carefully encoded phrases used over the breakfast table by Mr Windling in *The Truth* to mask his racism. Pratchett certainly avoided any suggestion that his fiction approached issues with a political or ideological stance. In an interview with the webzine *FTL* in 2005, he denied that such episodes as Nobby getting in touch with his 'female side' or the drag episodes in *Jingo* had any 'activist' elements, arguing that 'the stuff evolves from the characters'.[3] This, of course, does not deny that there was a consistent thread of tolerance and common decency running through his work, mixed with an equally consistent fury at unfairness and human moral self-deception.

In a series of short articles published in *The Discworld Chronicle* before the 1998 second Discworld Convention, Victoria Martin considered terms like Right, Good and Nice as they apply to the Discworld's characters, and the moral maps they indicate. According to Martin, this spectrum of qualities comes from the Stephen Sondheim musical *Into the Woods* (1986), much admired by Pratchett. Arguing that Jack the Giant-killer should be handed over to the giant's wife who is seeking revenge, a witch justifies her case with the words 'I'm not Nice, I'm not Good, I'm just Right'.[4] These terms – which also cropped up in internet newsgroups devoted to Pratchett's works and to which he himself posted – are therefore neither mutually inclusive nor fit conveniently into a comforting ethical framework, which makes Pratchett's characterisation deeper, both as comedy and broader commentary.

Janet Brennan Croft extends this analysis in an article in *Mythlore* (2008).[5] While a perfectly 'positive' character may well be Right, Good *and* Nice (Martin cites Brutha of *Small Gods* as a possibility), the majority of Pratchett's 'good' characters embody, at most, only two of these virtues, and in a manner emphasising their inherent ambiguity. Granny Weatherwax, for instance, is Right, but not Nice: 'I've never claimed to be nice, just to be sensible' (*LL* 108). So is the Patrician Vetinari, who sees evil when he looks in his shaving mirror (*UA* 228) but who guides Ankh-Morpork on the road to stability from what, we see in *Night Watch*, is a combination of despotism and chaos. Vimes increasingly combats his own darkness. His pursuit of Carcer into the past shows him that a good cop carries within him the potentiality of a bad cop. 'What you were [...] was not the beast. You didn't have to do what it wanted' (*NW* 358). Carrot in his turn may be 'Good', but his 'Goodness' is that of the Rightful King: charismatic, but implicitly authoritarian. In *Jingo* he organises the delinquent street youth of Ankh-Morpork into football teams and teaches them Wolf Cubs chants. His assumption that people want to follow his example sounds naïve but the conversations between Carrot and Vetinari in *Men at Arms*, in which Carrot argues that 'people should do things because an officer tells them. They shouldn't do it just because Corporal Carrot says so' suggests that Carrot is well aware of his status (*MAA* 281).

While 'Niceness' might be seen as soppiness or wishful thinking – Magrat, who 'thinks you can lead your life as if fairy stories work and folk songs are really true' (*LL* 36) is central here – it does not preclude moving towards a darker element. Magrat is initially deemed by her elders too dim to understand the nature of Elves, because her sentimental longing for them is based upon misunderstanding what words describing them – 'glamorous', 'enchanting' 'terrific' – actually mean. When she understands that Elves project glamour, weave enchantment and inspire terror, she can outgrow her soppy persona and don the armour of the legendary Queen Ynci. Verence, Croft argues, becomes less 'Nice' in *Carpe Jugulum* as he begins to see his 'people' as subjects to be moulded, inviting vampires into his kingdom as part of a mistaken project of engaging with 'the modern world community'.[6] Nanny Ogg may be 'Nice' in a different way to Magrat, through her jolly bawdiness and conviviality, but the in-laws she terrorises might have a different opinion. As she admits: 'I'm only nice compared to Esme' (*M* 171). She is 'unexpectedly ruthless' when confronting the Horned King in *Lords and Ladies*.[7]

Magrat's successor Agnes Nitt deals with her own innate 'Niceness' by (unconsciously) creating 'the part of you that wants to do all the things you don't dare do, and thinks the thoughts you don't dare think' (*CJ* 67). The combination of Agnes's empathy and her more rebellious and transgressive alter ego Perdita is crucial to defeating the vampires in *Carpe Jugulum*. Pratchett's own claiming of Sam Vimes, when challenged to name a 'Nice' character, may seem paradoxical, but, Martin argues, Vimes knows his community in a way the cunningly manipulative Vetinari or the idealising Carrot does not. Aware of their faults and vices, he nevertheless cares about them.[8] In this way, he is also, like Granny Weatherwax, *Right*. 'Rightness respects the individual as a moral agent and never descends to treating him as an object'.[9] Granny denies the moral 'shades of grey' put forward by Mightily Oats as he grapples with the various dogmas of Omnianism. 'There's no greys, only white that's got grubby', Granny states firmly (*CJ* 210). Vorbis in *Small Gods* and Carcer in *Night Watch*, as well as Cox in *Nation*, are among Pratchett villains who treat people as *things*. Echoing Mightily Oats's theological language, this is *sin*: the starting point of the 'worse crimes' the young priest tries to point to. And while Vorbis, Carter and Cox are outright evil, there is subtle discomfort in the way the thoroughly Nice Glenda, in *Unseen Academicals*, comes to understand (fortunately in time) that treating someone as a *thing* is precisely what she is doing as she worries about her assistant Juliet's career as a model and realises that '*as soon as she found anything difficult you took it away and did it yourself*' (*UA* 253).

A similar spectrum linking Cleverness, Skill and Knowledge could be developed. At Discworld's heart are the Clever wizards – 'clever', as Susan remarks in *Hogfather*, 'isn't the same as sensible'

(*H* 132). Perhaps the most overtly stereotyped characters in the series, they are 'what everyone knows' about tradition-ridden academics claiming authority but lacking practicality, who use jargon to cover the fact that they don't really understand what they are saying. Hived off in their Ivory Tower, neutralised by the Patrician's manipulative politics, they have become the most slapstick of the characters. While Archchancellor Mustrum Ridcully develops from a buffoon to a crafty manager who, like Vetinari, values stability, only the increasingly important Ponder Stibbons actually wants to think about things. In *Lords and Ladies* and *The Last Continent* Ponder is Reader in Invisible Writings, using a magical library to study those books which have not been written yet: a wonderful metaphor for someone who wants to articulate something which has not as yet been articulated.

In contrast, we have Skilful characters. These include members of the Guilds, such as the Assassins of the early chapters of *Pyramids*. They are practical, unlike the primarily theoretical wizards: good at a particular task. Practicality itself is not an unmixed blessing. Death is, more than anyone, an expert. He speaks to Jason Ogg the blacksmith '[a]s one craftsman to another' (*LL* 5). In *Mort*, he has a trade – even an apprentice. But his horizons are limited by that trade. While he knows more about the eternal verities than anyone else on the Discworld – after all, he is one of them – he has no idea about why people behave as they do. Verence is Skilful as a Fool, being trained in telling unfunny jokes; and his fumbling attempts to become as Skilful in being a King (or a husband) are part of the humour of the character. Linking Clever and Skilful are such characters as Bloody Stupid Johnson, an unparalleled genius of a craftsman who constantly gets things wrong in the design stage, and Leonard of Quirm, unable to believe that the thought-experiment weapons and vehicles he designs could actually be used in warfare.

Finally, there are Knowledgeable characters such as Granny Weatherwax or the Librarian, direct foils to the wizards, who could not function effectively without them. The distinction between them and the Skilful is that they are aware of subtler social nuances than the workings of their specific trades. Witches are broadly Knowledgeable, although Magrat as junior Witch, learning a craft, starts off as Skilful. She works, at first, literally by the book, not quite understanding that witchcraft is as much about understanding and occasionally guiding people (Granny's 'headology') as it is about 'doing things'.

The Librarian understands the dynamics of L-Space. It is, however, difficult to place him on a moral spectrum, unlike the equally Knowledgeable Granny Weatherwax. She is very much the centre of the novels in which she appears (including the Tiffany Aching sequence where she mentors Tiffany). Role and story have the potential to trap us, but at the heart of Granny's conviction is her knowledge that moral choice defeats narrative causality. This means taking on responsibility, and it is responsibility and choice which is at the heart of Pratchett's ethical framework, as Farah Mendlesohn points out, drawing upon a wide range of Discworld novels to argue that even Rincewind's 'cowardice' is a refusal to be complicit in the way the world works, while Granny's rigidity masks compassion, and Vimes understands mercy.[10]

CHOICE

Granny, we know from *Witches Abroad*, could be evil should she choose to be. In *Carpe Jugulum*, called to a difficult childbirth, she refuses to step aside from her responsibility as healer to allow a man the agonising choice of whether wife or child should die. Right or wrong, the choice is hers. Sam Vimes could let loose the 'beast' within him, but chooses not to. The tension between Vimes and Vetinari offers similar foregrounding of role and responsibility, although their approaches are different. Vimes wants to believe that there is scope for fairness in an imperfect world. Vetinari, on the other hand identifies the complexities of Ankh-Morpork and surrounding countries as a brutal 'state of nature', only controllable by a ruler skilled in manipulating and dividing the forces against him. Though Vimes believes in 'the good people and the bad people', '[t]here are, always and only, the bad people, but some of them are on opposite sides' (*GG* 302). At first, Vimes considers Vetinari's analysis nihilist. But by *Snuff* Vimes also sees the face of evil in his shaving mirror (*Sn* 295).

His final encounter with Carcer in *Night Watch* is also his confrontation with the side of his nature that makes him not simply a policeman/'polis'-man, a 'man of the city', but a warring animal in the Hobbesian conflict of all against all. Here, we are far from the early novels. Nevertheless, Vetinari refuses to be an arbitrarily merciless tyrant (except perhaps to mime artists), and Vimes refuses to allow himself to override his commitment to the rules of law. Whether this takes them out of the category of 'bad people' into 'good people' is precisely the moral argument the author wants us to face, for this confusion of categories is universal. The low-level resentment and vindictiveness of the Elucidated Brethren in *Guards! Guards* is one thing. More troubling is the 'normal, kindly family man' drinking his tea from mugs inscribed 'The World's Greatest Daddy' typical of the workforce of Vorbis's torturers in *Small Gods* (*SG* 15). Even Makepeace in *Snuff*, a minor character portrayed as a Good, if somewhat pathetic man, is complicit in the treatment of the goblins. Vimes's arrival allows him to speak up. His former silence is because he cares for his wife, though she is 'a rather foolish woman who does appear to worship things like titles' (*Sn* 361). He still shares in collective guilt.

In perhaps less dramatic form, the Tiffany Aching series returns to questions of responsibility and choice. 'Them as can do, has to do for them as can't. And someone has to speak up for them as has no voices' (*WFM* 196). Tiffany's grandmother, Granny Aching, was an unofficial witch in a land which, technically, has no witches. Tiffany's own ability as a witch causes tension in her community, and some social embarrassment within her loving family. Her father is proud of her, but it is a 'proud *puzzlement*' (*ISWM* 36). At times he is unsure whether it is daughter or witch whom he is questioning.

The morality and ethics of race, class, sexuality/gender and religion are also examples of where later Discworld and non-series novels once again show deeper and more nuanced mapping of the 'fantastic' secondary world upon the actual issues of the 'real' world. This is particularly the case in the children's books. Dodger, for example, is a rogue, but an honest rogue. His pity for Sweeney Todd, driven murderously insane by his wartime experiences, and the street children he feeds – in fact, his initial impulse to intervene when a young woman is being beaten – all mark Dodger as kind and generous. Although he always says this is self-preservation, it is, as near as may be, altruism. Johnny Maxwell evaluates and articulates the moral ambiguity of the 'many worlds' model of the multiverse, where what you do in your 'present' changes the future. The multiverse of possible futures becomes Johnny's guide to do the right thing rather than a way of adjusting plot: 'Everything we do changes the future, all the time. So we ought to do what's right' (*JATB* 98).

IDENTITIES

Throughout the Discworld series the relationships between its multi-species inhabitants satirised racial issues, particularly through the long-running thread involving the recruitment of Discworld's so-called 'ethnic minorities' (*GG* 45) into the watch. This begins with the recruitment of Carrot (actually a human adopted by dwarfs) in *Guards! Guards!* and the Dwarf Cuddy, the Troll Detritus, and the Werewolf Angua in *Men at Arms*. Vimes's initial distrust grows into acceptance through his equal-opportunities dislike of every species, including his own. *Jingo* develops this focus when a territorial dispute between Klatch and Ankh-Morpork threatens to disrupt relationships between Ankh-Morporkians and its sizeable population of immigrant and immigrant-descended Klatchians. Fred Colon's education at 'the University of What Some Bloke In the Pub Told Me' enables him to opine authoritatively to Nobby that Klatchians are 'not the same colour as what we are', and that their contribution to mathematics is 'nothing' (as they invented the concept of zero). Nobby's naïve but logical response 'like [...] they viciously attack you while cowardly running away after tasting cold steel?' (*J* 28–29) undermines Ankh-Morporkian racism, as does the more sophisticated exchange between the Klatchian Prince Khufarah and Vimes when each understands the significance of the insult 'towelhead', a term only Vimes among the Ankh-Morporkians is honest enough to explain (*J* 52). By the end of the novel, in which a peace is brokered by Vimes and his Klatchian equivalent 71-Hour Ahmed, even Fred Colon thinks that a pub called the Klatchian's Head has something morally dubious about it (*J* 283). The 'head' in *Jingo* is wooden. In *Snuff*, there is, to Vimes's consternation, an actual Goblin's head displayed in the village pub. The figurative Klatchian's head is a symbol of supremacy, but of a war long ago. The contemporary reality of an actual goblin's head cannot be so easily escaped.

Pratchett's most incisive writing on this issue is, perhaps, *Johnny and the Bomb*. Johnny and his friends find themselves in 1940s Blackbury. Yo-less, portrayed as amusing because he does not conform to stereotypes of 'being black', is referred to by a shopkeeper as 'Sambo'. Palpably hurt and angry, he is ushered out of the shop only to be condescended to by Kirsty, who excuses the woman's unthinking racism as only reflecting her upbringing; 'You people can't expect us to rewrite history, you know' (*JATB* 86) The exchange is comic – Yo-less returns the same words to her when a policeman later addresses her as 'little lady', reflecting the unthinking *sexism* of the times – but chilly. As Pratchett notes through Johnny's understanding of his friend's reaction, the impersonal coldness of 'you people' is worse than the original slur.

Vimes's observation that laws are made for those who are neither 'those who made the law' nor the 'incorrigibly lawless' (*FOC* 162) is, according to Mendlesohn, a stance rarely seen in much fantasy literature, in which social mobility tends to acceptance of the status quo or at best ignoring the fact that there is a class issue.[11] Although Vimes rises from street urchin to Duke, he remains aware that his ascent is due to Vetinari's manipulation on the one hand and Sybil's love on the other. His cynical disbelief that 'others deserve either their poverty or their wealth'[12] remains the same throughout. His distrust of the aristocratic class he marries into causes Sybil to exclaim 'you're determined to be your very own class enemy' (*S* 144). Yet he does not romanticise the working class, unlike Reg Shoe's parroting revolutionary slogans in *Night Watch*. Vimes's upbringing in the Shades, the slum area of Ankh-Morpork, confirms his cynicism. His adversary in *Guards! Guards!*, Lupine Wonse, comes from the same background, establishing himself as the gang-leader's lieutenant 'allowed to stay because he's the one who comes up with all the clever ideas' (*GG* 43) and working his way up to the position of Vetinari's secretary. As Supreme Grand Master of the Elucidated Brethren of the Ebon Night, Wonse exploits the petty grievances of people whose sense of oppression comes not from any class identification but from complaining neighbours, nagging wives and relatives who have more expensive coaches. The common people are 'nothing special', Vimes observes in *Feet of Clay* (269), no different from the rich and powerful except that they are *not* rich and powerful and, therefore need the law on their side.

The breakfast-table conversations in William de Worde's lodging house reveal small-minded people who comment that the city is getting too crowded but 'no offence meant' if so-called 'outsiders' find their remarks offensive (*TT* 95, 188). The significant difference, though, between Mr Windling of the lodging house, and Tuttle Scrope, one of the 'concerned citizens' who want 'a return to the values and traditions that made the city great' (*TT* 238) is that Windling is a powerless bigot and the 'citizens' are aristocrats (including de Worde's father) who have enlisted the New Firm of Mr Tulip and Mr Pin to frame Vetinari for murder, with Scrope the figurehead they plan to install as the next Patrician. The world, as Pratchett says in the beginning of the novel, belongs to those powerful enough to look at a half-empty glass and say: 'Excuse me? This is my glass? I don't think so. My glass was full! And it was a bigger glass!', as opposed to 'the other type of person, who has a broken glass [...] or who had no glass at all' (*TT* 25). De Worde, who establishes Ankh-Morpork's first newspaper, is both ally and adversary of Vimes: ally because he is concerned with truth and law over class privilege, adversary because his defence of the 'big truth' includes 'journalistic surveillance of the police'.[13] He too is also 'his own class enemy', in this case, against his father, a man whose use of the term 'lesser races' colours in the picture William describes to the dwarf Gunilla Goodmountain (*TT* 182). William himself is a liberal trying (with some difficulty) to overcome his un-liberal background, nervously protesting to Otto Chriek, the vampire iconographer that he is 'very much at home with other species'. Otto perceptively notices that William 'was not brought up nice but he tries to be a nice person' (*TT* 287). William does, in the end, play his aristocratic 'privilege' ('private law') card to make his father leave the city in return for him not revealing the truth, an action which does not endear him to Vimes but which the Patrician understands as part of the network of manipulations and deals which enables a complex society to function.

Just as *The Truth* satirises 'respectable' small-mindedness, *Unseen Academicals* shows the deadly cosiness of community. The identification with the collective which football allows is transcendent, but it is also the 'shove', the mindless violence of the crowd that keeps people in their place and gives power to psychopaths like Andy Shank. The novel's other image, the 'crab bucket' ('you have to grab life or drop back into the crab bucket', as Pepe observes (*UA* 159), comes from a phenomenon observed by Verity Pushpram, the fishmonger (Nobby's *amour* in other novels) when she pulls out a crab from a bucket to find three others hanging onto it. Glenda at once understands that any crab trying to escape is pulled back, an observation which applies to her life and, especially, to her friend Juliet who could spend her working life as Glenda's rather dim assistant or take advantage of the opportunity to be a model for the range of dwarf clothing devised by the louche but kindly Madame Sharn. 'Practically everything my mum ever told me, that's crab bucket. Practically everything I've ever told Juliet, that's crab bucket too' (*UA* 218).

If many Pratchett characters wrestle with their class identities, sexual/gender stereotypes are part of the comedy for others. The internet journal *Gender Forum* issued a special issue on Pratchett in 2015, arguing that 'Pratchett's humorous writing presents strict gender norms as being both restrictive and surmountable, and his fiction easily and clearly subverts gender and genre-specific stereotypes'.[14] Jacob M. Held, in an essay published in *Philosophy and Terry Pratchett* (2014), notes that the sexless golems in *Going Postal* default to 'Mr', but argues that 'Gladys' (who begins to dress and act like a stereotypical woman) is an example of how gender is performative. Although rather overlooking the music-hall joke at the centre here – Gladys is deemed 'female' because the prim and proper Miss Maccalariat cannot have a *male* golem cleaning the ladies toilets – Held shows how the developing jokes about Gladys' growing 'femininity' do lead to a growing realisation that such femininity *is* performance. Later, he argues that in *Monstrous Regiment* Sergeant Jackrum's performance as a man in the Borogravian army leads to the point that he 'can no longer even fathom living as a woman' and has to be considered as 'a transgender woman who transitioned into a man some time ago and only now fully realizes and accepts it'.[15] Some years after his death, there were attempts to enlist Pratchett among 'gender-critical' opponents to transgender issues, but these were vehemently rebutted by many of his friends and (especially) his daughter.

Katherine Lashley offers a study of *Monstrous Regiment* noting the comic effects produced by the way the young women joining the Borogravian army try to disguise their femininity by imitating the other soldiers – in effect, copying *other women* who are imitating men; and in the behaviour of Lieutenant Blouse (the commander of Polly Perks's unit) who adopts Polly's idea to infiltrate an enemy stronghold disguised as women but believes that his 'men' would give their masculinity away far too easily, and therefore adopts, himself, a pantomime-dame disguise as a washerwoman. Lashley, in considering what is actually happening here, raises the question of gender as performance and whether Blouse's over-exaggerated portrayal of femininity (big breasts, domestic chores, swaying hips and bursting into tears) that so easily persuades the enemy soldiers is an indication that men have delineated a code of conduct and appearance for women. If so, when the *women* (passing as men) need to 'disguise' themselves as women, they seem to fail: 'they mock the idea of womanhood set up by the patriarchy, because they cannot perfectly imitate the ideal woman'.[16]

Some of this 'feminism' may stand in incongruous contrast to the comic-postcard depiction of other women, such as the way Mrs Whitlow's generous bosom causes consternation to the Senior Wrangler in *The Last Continent*. But Pratchett himself seemed firmly committed to subverting gender stereotypes. He began questioning gender through his depiction of dwarfs, the bearded, aggressive, secretive beings that stem from Tolkien's Dwarves. In Tolkien, Dwarf women are few, rarely seen in public. Pratchett's Dwarfs are physically indistinguishable, the joke being that dwarf courtship begins with trying to discover what gender the other dwarf is. Cheery in *Feet of Clay* is a dwarf identified by Angua, presumably through her werewolf senses, as female. Being unigender, she tells Angua, works well, but up to a point. While there are 'plenty of women in this town that'd love to do things the dwarf way', Cheery points out that dwarf women can do anything the men do so long as it is 'only what the men do' (*FOC* 78). Cheery *wants* to be 'feminine', wear colourful clothes and makeup, but dwarfs, as we see in *The Fifth*

Elephant, Thud! and *Feet of Clay* distrust such manifestations of femininity.

A second gender thread involves Nobby Nobbs of the watch. In *Jingo*, Nobby asks an embarrassed Angua for advice about his 'sexual nature', by which he means that he wants to settle down with a permanent relationship. The scene, as with so much about Nobby, introduced as a pilferer and skiver 'with a certain resemblance to a chimpanzee who never got invited to tea parties' (*GG* 40) is verbal slapstick based upon incongruity and grotesque character. (Nobby is a wearer of flamboyant clothes in his off-duty hours, and one of his hobbies is folk-dancing.) His 'I mean, if you want a thing done properly then...' hints at the kind of actual *sex* he is getting (*J* 39). Later, his cross-dressing as 'exotic dancer' Beti plays with a number of stereotypes but results in Nobby being on the receiving end of male sexism after only ten minutes as a 'woman'. In *Thud!*, Nobby is in a relationship with Tawneee, a pole-dancer so beautiful that no man has ever dared ask her out before. Angua, Cheery and Sally, the new vampire recruit to the Watch, put Tawneee right, on a 'girls night out', about exactly *why* men like to watch her dance in a strip club, and boost her self-esteem so that she can aim higher than Nobby. Pratchett is manipulating stereotypes rather than seriously analysing gender roles. In *Snuff*, though, when Tears of the Mushroom takes a shine to Nobby, this is not played for laughs. The joke is rather on Sam Vimes, who is told 'it's not our business' when he expresses doubt about it: 'There's a troll and a dwarf in Lobbin Clout who have set up home together, so I've heard. Good for them, I say, it's their business and definitely not ours' (*S* 340).

Pratchett's comedy tends to avoid actual sex, although it is clear that Carrot and Angua in the Watch series are a sexually active couple, Sam and Sybil seem happy with their sex life, and Nanny Ogg's sexually promiscuous past (and probably present, once she meets Casanunda) is constantly referred to. The Seamstress's Guild ('ladies of negotiable affection') is part of the social/political network of Ankh-Morpork. Its head, Rosie Palm, is one of the senior Guild leaders. Heterosexuality is very much the norm, although the existence of Tuttle Scrope's shop selling 'rubber work, and ... feathers ... and whips ... and ... little jiggly things', and the specialist 'tastes' hinted at by Mrs Palm suggests that sexuality is more imaginative in Ankh-Morpork than in most fantasyworlds (*TT* 289; *FOC* 154). Certainly, Discworld is one of the few fantasyworlds to admit the presence of contraception, in the form of the 'rubber goods' purveyed by Wallace Sonky in *The Fifth Elephant*. The sexuality of Pepe, Madame Sharn's partner in *Unseen Academicals*, is kept ambiguous for a while. 'Pepe is [...] Pepe', said Madame. 'And there is no changing him, as it were, or her. Labels are such unhelpful things, I feel' (*UA* 144). Sexuality among the wizards of Unseen University is sublimated in favour of their 'occult' powers, although some wizards harbour hidden urges concerning Mrs Whitlow, the Housekeeper. Archchancellor Ridcully's bluff acceptance of homosexuality – 'People make such a fuss. Anyway, in my opinion there's not enough love in the world' (*UA* 190) – might be seen to be the worldly tolerance of someone firmly-enough established in their own skin to *be* tolerant. But Ridcully's stubborn shrewdness makes him an interesting-enough character to have developed into one of the series' 'viewpoint' characters.

RELIGION

Although Pratchett was himself a humanist – he was a patron of the British Humanist Association – he seems to have accepted the value of religion as story so long as it remains story. The different belief-systems that make up the nature of the Hogfather – the sacrificed King whose death brings about the rising of the sun in midwinter, the jolly giver of gifts to children – are not, as Susan learns, fantasies to make life bearable but practice in believing 'little lies' so that we can believe the 'big ones' such as Justice, Mercy, Duty (*H* 270). Gods are different from creators. The Discworld's creator, as might be expected when Rincewind encounters him in *Eric*, is a slightly dodgy specialist. ('I don't contract for the big stuff, the stars, the gas giants, the pulsars and so on'). Gods are something of an afterthought (*E* 92, 96). Discworld has them, but they are, like Death and the Hogfather, anthropomorphic personifications created by human belief, and include Bilious, the Oh God of Hangovers, and Anoia, the goddess of things that get stuck in drawers, as well as those powerful gods for whom the Discworld inhabitants are counters in their games. Discworld's atheists such as Abraxas of Ephebe (*Small Gods*) are easy targets for thunderbolts. Om in *Small Gods* hovers on the edge of belief, which in Discworld-god terms means his power is weakened by the fact that only Brutha truly *believes* in him. Vorbis, not exactly High Priest but head of a complicated and cruel superstructure which enforces dogma, is determined to stamp out the heresy that (in a clever echo of Galileo's apocryphal remark when recanting his theory of heliocentrism) 'the turtle moves'. His attempted punishment/sacrifice of Brutha does result in Om's manifestation in a crescendo of 'belief', but not in the way he imagines. Brutha, the long-promised 'prophet', is entitled to speak for Om, and his commandments are uttered in the form of a dialogue, even a bargain, with the god. If there is a moral code to be followed, it is: 'I think ... you should do things because they're right. Not because gods say so. They might say something different another time'. And if there are commandments, Brutha says to Om – 'No commandments unless you obey them too' (*SG* 249).

The change in Omnianism can be seen in *Carpe Jugulum* in the figure of Mightily Oats, a troubled young priest unsure how to deal with his religion's multitude of schisms and viewpoints. To return to Martin's schematic, Oats may not be *right* in either his doubts or beliefs, but when he burns his holy book to keep Granny alive, we know he is *good*. Oats's fellow-Omnian Constable Visit of the Watch is also mocked in *Feet of Clay* and *Jingo*, but gently. There is no suggestion that he harms people, although his habit of thrusting religious tracts upon them may irritate. Pratchett's own humanism seems to allow the dynamic within belief in *Nation* and the Bromeliad trilogy. Ataba debates with Mau about gods who seem to have abandoned their people. Ataba points out to 'demon boy' Mau that he, too has lost family in the tsunami. He envies Mau's capacity for rage, but cannot give in to it: 'we call upon the silent gods, because they are better than the darkness' (*N* 259), Similarly, while Gurder and Angalo argue about whether nomes should trust in Arnold Bros (est. 1905)'s guidance or admit that they have achieved their escape from the Store through their own efforts, each have the interests of the nomes at the forefront of their imagination.

While religion, for Pratchett, is a constructed set of beliefs, he is not interested in entirely deconstructing it. The jokes about the way nomes read signs like 'Bargains Galore' or 'Prices Slashed' as evidence of benevolent or demonic entities, or 'If You Do Not See What You Require, Please Ask' as proof that a deity will answer prayers, subvert religious belief. However, Pratchett also subverts religious *dis*belief by suggesting that such stories may be necessary. Angalo, convinced that the nomes escaped without divine intervention, is still unable to let go of his religious education. 'Gurder was not certain, not entirely certain, that Arnold Bros (est. 1905) really existed, and Angalo wasn't entirely certain that he didn't' (*Di* 36). The ultimate joke, perhaps, is that Arnold Bros (Frank W. and Arthur: two human entrepreneurs) *did* create the store – and, according to the account of Grandson Richard in *Wings*, at least half-believed in the existence of little people behind the walls. It is indeed Gurder who wants to make sense of things, and who stays behind when the mothership is discovered to help find other scattered nome groups. The problem is Nisodemus, who wants to abandon Masklin's plan to carry on with their 'escape', and to rebuild the store as a 'sign' to Arnold Bros (est. 1905) who would return and 'smite' the humans. Nisodemus's scheme is, like many ideologically utopian plans, not necessarily *evil*, but good ideas warped and inverted: 'ones you couldn't sensibly argue with, because a good idea was still in there somewhere' (*Di* 61).

After *Small Gods*, the Bromeliad and *Nation*, *Monstrous Regiment* is perhaps Pratchett's most extensive debate about religion. Borogravia is subject to the dictates of the god Nuggan, who lists longer and more chaotically random lists of Abominations. The oppressed population turn in their acts of devotion and prayers to Borogravia's Duchess, who may in fact be no longer alive, but their belief, and especially that of Wazzer, the most damaged of the recruits, allows her to manifest as a goddess. Here, Pratchett seems to be approaching Marx's often misinterpreted portrayal of religion as the 'opium of the people' – not, or not *only*, outright illusion but necessary (in the present social conditions of humanity) soothing of suffering. The Duchess's plea to her believers is to fight Nuggan, the embodiment of 'all your ignorance and pettiness and malicious stupidity' but – significantly – to 'let [...] me [...] go!' (*MW* 318).

Mr Tulip in *The Truth* is equally damaged. He does not worry about 'religion stuff' because he has his potato, he tells his fellow-thug, Mr Pin. Even if you have done really bad things, if you 'have your potato' and are really sorry, you have your chance at another life. Mr Tulip has picked up this debased and silly notion from a woman's chance remark as, in some forgotten war in a far-off country, they are cowering in fear from invading soldiers and a grubbed-up potato really will mean the difference between survival and starvation. He *believes*, remarks Death after Mr Tulip has been killed, but he does not believe in anything – certainly no concept like 'God' was ever presented to him. But as his memories of what he has done return to him, he realises that atonement involves much more than a potato and simply *saying* sorry. Redemption can only come if he faces up to what he has done. This acknowledgement, coupled with the continuing joke of his portrayal as an art connoisseur (his last words to Death include admiration of the craftwork on his scythe) becomes less grotesque humour and more a poignant reminder that, in the words of Death, he 'HAD SOMETHING IN HIM THAT COULD BE BETTER' (*TT* 289).

In contrast, Mr Pin claims redemption as a right. He kills his friend to prolong his own life and steals his potato. In his own confrontation with Death, he thinks that it is all a matter of superciliously waving his symbol around and faking sorrow. Pratchett is unforgiving to such sophistry. Death abides by the letter of the law, as Mr Pin gets the reincarnation he has demanded – as a potato whose destiny is the chip-pan.

The Amazing Maurice also explores religion and ethics, and the way story enables us to 'face the darkness'. Suddenly becoming intelligent self-aware beings, the rats must confront their nature. So does Maurice whose *own* nature as a cat is to be a predator upon rats. Early on, one of the rats has qualms about whether taking a coach whose driver has run away from a highwayman is *stealing*. Another asks whether their activity of continuing their rat-behaviour of stealing food and damaging property so that the 'stupid-looking kid' can pretend to pipe the 'plague of rats' away is morally right (*AM* 22). Maurice himself, though he believes that the foolish are there to be fooled, recalls how his own development of self-awareness has led him not to eat anyone who could talk. Now rats can think, Dangerous Beans tells their leader Hamnpork, they have to be ethical. Thinking, and being able to imagine possibilities – including the possibility of something that may threaten them – allows them to control their fears: 'Learning to face the shadows outside helps us to fight the shadows inside. And you can control *all* the darkness' (*AM* 45).

The rats also possess a book which becomes a 'sacred text'. The picture-book *Mr Bunnsy Has An Adventure*, in which animals are seen wearing clothes and living human-like lives, seems to the rats to be a utopian vision of a bright future for them. And the 'the Big Rat Deep Under The Ground' speculation of how the rats came to be (*AM* 59) is, like the nomes' Arnold Bros (est. 1905), a speculation to explain their existence, to answer the question 'who works out what's right? Where does "right" and "wrong" come from?' (*AM* 91). But the rats' position, as expressed by Dangerous Beans when they argue about what they should do to an 'un-uplifted' rat, is: 'We can think. We can think about what we do. We can pity the innocent one who means us no harm' (*AM* 103). We are back with moral choice and responsibility, and while Pratchett is clear that Ataba's belief in his gods, or Gurder's faith in Arnold Bros (est. 1905) does not make them bad people, he wrote to Humanists UK: 'I hope it doesn't escape readers of *Maurice* that the rats develop a moral society before speculating that there's a Big Rat who created everything'.[17]

8

Pratchett and his Audiences

The announcement of Terry Pratchett's death appeared in the form of a tweet in the famous block capitals: 'AT LAST, SIR TERRY, WE MUST WALK TOGETHER'.[1] Readers throughout the world got the joke, and the grief and laughter were genuine.

Because of his training as a journalist, Pratchett was aware that he is writing for an audience, writing to be *read*; that a piece of writing, in a very real sense, did not even *exist* until it was being read. 'Some of the best literature that has been written has been written by people who were well aware that there are readers out there'; 'You're always aware of the people on the other side of the page'.[2] His success was very much because he has, in fact, various audiences. Many of his readers, of course, would have begun reading him at a young age, perhaps in their early teens as the Discworld books began to appear in the 1980s, and stayed until *The Shepherd's Crown* in 2015. They would have grown up with his works, reading and re-reading them as their own tastes and habits changed as they matured, experiencing his early books differently with the passing years (and in some cases finally understanding jokes that had passed over their heads). They would have bought and read the Bromeliad and Johnny Maxwell books as adults *because* they were by a writer they enjoyed. Other readers would, as children or teenagers, come across the children's books, especially the Carnegie Award-winning *Amazing Maurice* in the library, and only then sought others. As with many other popular sf/fantasy writers, fanzines would be devoted to his work (*The Wizard's Knob*, for instance, published fourteen issues 1993 to 2000), and the possibilities of the internet in discussion and compiling resources linking a wide variety of readers would be developed with the *Annotated Pratchett Files* and the inclusive *lspace.org* sites, which still remain as essential sources of information about Pratchett's works.

Pratchett cemented his love for science fiction by writing for fanzines and attending conventions such as the 1964 RePetercon (the UK national Easter SF convention) in Peterborough, where the 15-year-old schoolboy, already a published writer with his story in *Science Fantasy*, met other writers and made at least one lifelong friend.[3] His writing, as has been noted in other chapters, came out of the shared subculture of fandom, and for some years he tried to keep a foot in this culture. Although he remarks in an address to Noreascon, the 2004 World Science Fiction Convention, that he was a 'fan, a real convention-going fan, for only maybe three years' (*ASOTK* 57) until marriage and a demanding job took him away, his experience of British sf conventions in the 1960s, where writers and their readers mingled not always as professionals and fans but through a shared love of their reading, enabled him to develop a recognisable voice in which he could communicate with the fandom which grew around his books. He took advantage of the opportunities the development of the internet offered him, engaging with fan groups such as *alt.fan.pratchett* and their discussions, reaching out to his audience in book signings, where he would thank them for the money in a self-deprecating performative fashion which went down well, although it rather troubled fellow writer Christopher Priest in his review of Wilkins's biography.[4] In particular, his guest of honour appearances at conventions, especially the regular Discworld conventions, offered him an opportunity to mix, although as Paul Kincaid noted in a response to Priest's review referring to his own encounter with Pratchett at an Australian convention, the sense of being 'on display' often 'warped the reality around him', when he wanted simply to socialise with people he knew.[5] His relationship with his fans (to many of whom he was 'Pterry' – stemming from the Egyptian 'silent P' joke in many of the names in *Pyramids*, in which two of the characters were Pteppic/Teppic and Ptraci) is an interesting example of fan culture, and Jakob Löfgre, in a piece in *Folklore*, considers the performance/staged narratives of a Hogswatch celebration in Wincanton, Somerset (then part of a regular series of such celebrations hosted in part by the Discworld Emporium, specialising in Discworld memorabilia and spin-off products) in the context of fan/folklore studies.[6] During punishing schedules of national and international tours as books were published, and in speeches at the Discworld conventions, his relationship with his readers was close. He took answering fan mail seriously as 'part of the whole process' remembering himself as the young fan who had received a reply from J. R. R. Tolkien thanking him for his appreciation of *Smith of Wooton Major*, and believing, according to his assistant Rob Wilkins, that 'his success derived in some vital way from his accessibility'.[7]

His enduring success, however, came from his ability to appeal to audiences beyond a single subculture. In a 1993 essay for *The Author* about his fan mail, Pratchett noted the 'quite unfair' term for his fans, the 'Kevins' ('one day the post included three letters all from boys called Kevin') but pointed out that '[m]any of them are female. Some of them are grandmothers' (*ASOTK* 73). Pratchett's first major public exposure was to the 'audience of well-read women' who heard *The Colour of Magic* serialised on BBC Radio 4's *Woman's Hour* in 1984, and '[i]t's worth pointing out, also, that the audience of well-read women loved what they heard'.[8] *Equal Rites* was similarly serialised. One demographic study of Pratchett's readership, carried out for a PhD thesis in 2007 and eliciting over 1,300 responses from a questionnaire sent out to recipients of the web-based fan newsletter *Discworld Monthly*, found that a majority (55%) of the respondents were female.[9]

Much of the critical response to Pratchett centres around the women in his fiction. Marion Rana's collection, *Terry Pratchett's Narrative Worlds*, begins with essays on the Witches (Alice Nuttall) and the gender issues raised by the character Angua in the Watch novels (Marion Rana). The online *Gender Forum* special issue on Pratchett was mentioned in the previous chapter, but useful comments on the novels up to *Monstrous Regiment* are made by the Australian author Tansy Rayner Roberts in a selection of self-published essays, *Pratchett's Women*, in which she engages with her own changing opinions over time, and draws attention to the way Pratchett, in his early novels, is 'mocking the semi-clad, bosomy fantasy women who traditionally reward the handsome hero with their sexy selves'[10] though only by re-creating that very cliché as he attempts to invert it. Yet he has also, especially in later novels, genuinely managed to explore and develop a range of female characters. Roberts's journey as a Pratchett fan, beginning as a young teenager ('when I was fourteen and reading the Discworld novels for the first time, I adored Conina and Ptraci and Ginger and totally wanted to be just like them when I grew up'[11]) progresses through multiple re-readings and various audio-book recordings, including books she disliked at the time of first reading, such as *Jingo* and *The Fifth Elephant* which she 'loathed [...] the first time around'[12] and, in particular, *Monstrous Regiment*. ('I don't have the excuse (as with my young adoration of Ginger and Ptraci) that it was my teenage self that took against this astoundingly feminist book. I was in my mid-twenties and (I thought) pretty clued in about the importance of women in fantasy.')[13] She also praises *Night Watch* as a book 'that got me excited about the Discworld and Pratchett's writing after a long dry spell of not loving his books any more'.[14]

Part of this 'dry spell' might have been a reaction to Josh Kirby's cover art, a feature of Discworld novels since the Corgi paperback edition of *The Colour of Magic* until *The Truth* in 2000. Much of the appeal of Discworld – certainly to fantasy readers, lay in Kirby's colourful covers, about which, however, Roberts writes 'Even when the writing in the Discworld books challenged and questioned the roles of female characters in fantasy, the original covers reinforced the clichés'.[15] Kirby was a successful and respected cover artist in a number of genres and styles before Discworld. One of his early commissions was the 1956 paperback edition of Ian Fleming's James Bond adventure *Moonraker*, and he had illustrated many of the classic sf/fantasy novels that the young Terry Pratchett would have read. His 'Discworld' work was many readers' first point of entry into Pratchett's world',[16] and the appeal of his 'cartoonish and often carnivalesque style'[17] with exaggerated and hectic activity spoke to a generation of fantasy readers in search of a sense of storytelling and detail which went beyond simple escapism. While his 'pink and bosomy cartoon women' also troubled readers like A. S. Byatt for a while,[18] his style, says Alton, succeeds in 'reflecting the frenetic energy of life on the Discworld [...] and they also reflect the layers of meaning one finds throughout Pratchett's prose'.[19]

After Kirby's death in 2001, Paul Kidby took over the artwork for the Discworld books. His style, more tuned to a realistic portrayal of characters and parody of famous paintings such as Rembrandt's *The Night Watch* (re-created on the cover of the Discworld novel echoing that title), reflected the quieter, sometimes darker progression of the sequence, although his vivid illustrations to *The Last Hero* were a tour de force that marked him as a successor to Kirby. Anne Hiebert Alton contrasts the 'feeling of dizziness, giddiness, or vertigo' in Kirby's art with Kidby's greater concern for verisimilitude and realistically imagined detail ('more whimsical overtones than actual whimsy') – what Kidby himself called 'a more grounded interpretation'.[20] Each artist contributed in different ways to the sense of wonder engendered by the text, and worked closely with Pratchett in doing so.

His popular character, the Librarian of Unseen University, and the jokes about L-Space and the power of books made him popular among many British librarians, although his active support of libraries, and education *through* libraries, moved this popularity beyond the joke. Pratchett at one point was certainly something of a cult figure among librarians, particularly those working with children and young people. His popularity could be put down to the fact that here were books which people of all ages could enjoy, which librarians could offer to young people with the feeling that they were allowing access to something both popular and worthy, which did not need 'promoting' because their audience had already discovered them, and which attracted into libraries people who would not otherwise enter and turned them into avid readers. But as important was the fact that with the Librarian, Pratchett had created a role model with whom librarians in the beleaguered 1990s could identify, whose muscles and fangs and hair-trigger temper meant that budget cuts were never on the agenda at Unseen University.

From *Terry Pratchett: Guilty of Literature*, published by the Science Fiction Foundation in 2000 (with an expanded second edition in 2004), there began to be serious critical examination of Pratchett as a writer. Much of this, partly as a reaction to success in the Carnegie awards, seemed to place him as a writer for children, or in the context of other writers for children. Rana's *Terry Pratchett's Narrative Worlds*, Peter Hunt's chapter in

Alternative Worlds in Fantasy Fiction (2005) and Caroline Webb's *Fantasy and the Real World in British Children's Literature* (2015) are, for example, published within the context of series devoted to children's literature. As some of his books for children and young adults are among his best, and many of the Discworld readers *were* young, this is not entirely unfair, although A. S. Byatt, in the foreword to *A Blink of the Screen*, is at pains to point out that 'my literary friends are often addicted as I am' to his works, and calls him 'wise and grown up' (*ABOTS* 12, 13).[21] The essays in Held and South's *Philosophy and Terry Pratchett*, and Michaud, *Discworld and Philosophy*, both published in popular culture and philosophy series, often use Pratchett as teaching texts, illustrating ways of thinking rather than closely and critically examining his literary qualities. For example, Ben Saunders examines issues of equality and economic resources by imagining scenarios based on Discworld characters.[22] When this works, as in this case, we find our reading of Pratchett illuminated. At times, as in many of the essays in Michaud's collection, the temptation to indulge in fannish imitation of Pratchett's style overwhelms the educational value. More general collections, such as Alton et al., *Discworld and the Disciplines*, offer illuminating pathways into Pratchett's work, and taken as a whole, the various essays in Justine Breton's edited collection, *Power and Society in Terry Pratchett's Discworld*, move away from the narrower focus of earlier criticism to explore the dynamics between the individual, political and social 'spheres' of the Discworld.

The multi-audience nature of Pratchett's readership has sometimes revealed fissures between these audiences and misunderstandings within them. The publication of *Guilty of Literature* (whose contributors included people with deep roots in the British fan culture) was met with some suspicion among fans who distrusted the very idea of literary criticism. A review in *Discworld Monthly* warned such readers to avoid the book, noting that 'the pieces range from fairly successful to utterly dire', with the half-hearted conclusion that '[i]t's not all dross, by any means'. Another more welcoming, but still ambivalent review, on the webzine *Green Man Review*, called the book 'readable in most places, and a welcome spur to discussion and re-reading even for those of us who don't dwell in academia'.[23] In a lengthy *Guardian* article on the popularity of fantasy following the success of the television adaptations of George R. R. Martin's *Game of Thrones*, the critic John Mullan (Professor of English at University College London), remarked that 'Fantasy's devotees must feel rueful as the critics now rush to [...] record their admiration of Terry Pratchett', later dubbed 'fantasy's licensed jester', and that 'many of Pratchett's readers must also be readers of fantasy fiction, able to relish the irreverent parody as well as the real thing'. This apparent opposition of the 'irreverent parody' and the 'real thing' was, to the blogger Maureen Kincaid Speller (a prominent critic in the sf/fantasy fields), a false distinction, based upon a category error: distinguishing 'Pratchett readers' and 'fantasy readers'. ('Possibly, just ever so possibly, fantasy readers read Pratchett, and Pratchett fans vice versa'.) Mullan's piece, she argued, as it went on to investigate the way Kazuo Ishiguro's *The Buried Giant* owed a debt to fantasy fiction which, in Mullan's words 'must seem overdue vindication of the genre', simply fell into the trap of assuming 'a cultural power struggle between fantasy fans and mainstream critics'.[24]

It is perhaps the fact that such arguments and different positions exist, rather than whether one or other of them is right or wrong, that cements Pratchett's position as a literary figure. As a writer who has sold in the region of 100 million books worldwide, he had, and still has, a readership which encounters his books in many different contexts. By the time of his death, he was a writer no interest-group could 'own'. Awards, OBE, and a knighthood, and especially his work for combatting Alzheimer's after his diagnosis, seemed to make Pratchett approach 'national treasure' status. The references to Dickens which began to appear in reviews may have been journalism rather than literary analysis, although *Dodger* and a considerable amount of Ankh-Morpork owed much to Dickens and Dickensian London, and certainly to the journalistic energy and social fury to be found in Dickens. It is certainly the case that Pratchett was a humourist with an increasingly angry conscience who for a short while was the most popular writer in the country.

This popularity led, inevitably, to moves to project Discworld and other series to audiences beyond the readers of books. Some, including *Amazing Maurice*, the Johnny Maxwell series, and several Discworld novels, have been filmed or televised, and there are many spin-off works such as play scripts, calendars, diaries guidebooks and maps produced in consultation and collaboration with Pratchett. Do we conclude that Discworld now exists, as do the worlds of *Star Wars*, *Star Trek*, *Doctor Who* and others, as a 'franchise', beyond the work of the originating creators? Pratchett strove to keep control of his creations. As far as 'merchandise' is concerned, he 'hated' most of the ideas pitched to him.[25] He made an exception, with the wide range of Discworld merchandise which has been built up over the years from Bernard and Isobel Pearson, who began working with Pratchett to produce material with Clarecraft in 1991 and since 2000 traded as the Discworld Emporium. He was determined to control, as far as possible, adaptations of his works. *The Watch* (BBC America, 2021), significantly 'inspired by' rather than based upon the City Watch series, was largely developed after Pratchett's death without input from his estate, but most adaptations were faithful within the limits of their medium. *Soul Music*, *Wyrd Sisters* and *The Amazing Maurice* were adapted as animations, while *The Colour of Magic* (incorporated with *The Light Fantastic*), *Hogfather* and *Going Postal* were successful live-action films. Stephen Briggs, after adapting *Wyrd Sisters* for his amateur drama club in 1991, received permission to adapt another twenty-four books. As well as publishing the play-texts, he narrated audio versions of many Pratchett novels and was responsible, working closely with Pratchett, for the compilation of *The Streets of Ankh-Morpork* and *The Discworld Mapp*, painted by Stephen Player. Briggs has so far published (since 1995) four editions of the *Discworld Companion*, the official 'encyclopedia' of Discworld and (since 1998) has collaborated with Pratchett in publishing numerous Discworld diaries and calendars, usually built around aspects of the Discworld such as the Guilds or geographical locations such as Lancre.

Alton's use of the geometrical term 'hypotrochoidal' as metaphor describing texts generated from within another text but existing both inside and outside it is possibly rather strained (it marks the curves inside and outside a circle drawn by a point attached to a smaller circle rolling on its inside). But it seems to be useful to describe texts published in the 'real' world 'as from' within the Discworld – *Where's My Cow, The World of Poo, Nanny Ogg's Cookbook* as well as the maps, handbooks, calendars and other 'publications that have been generated from and appear within the Discworld multiverse and have a kind of simultaneous resonance'.[26] Such associated material – the maps, the calendars, the jigsaws, posters and figurines – are part of the 'mapping' of Discworld and an important aspect of how it has become, for many of Pratchett's readers, an imaginative and highly visual shared world. However, this 'cottage industry' has operated with the approval and sometimes direct involvement of Pratchett himself, and now continues via his assistant Rob Wilkins and daughter Rhianna, herself a writer. At the centre are the books, and Pratchett's own writing, and this will remain firmly established.

Notes

1. INTRODUCTION

1 Extracts from the Late Review programme shown in the BBC2 Back in Black programme: 'Back in Black (HD): For fans of the late Sir Terry Pratchett', *You Tube*, 11 February 2017, https://www.youtube.com/watch?v=UXQDV4RIwg0 (accessed 10 February 2024).

2 Rob Wilkins, *Terry Pratchett: A Life with Footnotes: The Official Biography* (London: Doubleday, 2022), 277.

3 Marc Burrows, *The Magic of Terry Pratchett* (Barnsley: Pen and Sword, 2020), 208.

4 Boris Johnson, 'Rich Imagination of Discworld's Doyen', *Daily Telegraph*, 11 May 1998, 34.

5 Terry Pratchett, 'Imaginary Worlds, Real Stories', *Folklore* 111:2 (Oct. 2000), 159.

6 Terry Pratchett, *A Slip of the Keyboard* (London: Doubleday, 2014), 163.

7 A. S. Byatt, 'Foreword' to Terry Pratchett, *A Blink of the Screen* (London: Doubleday, 2012), 12, 13.

8 Jonathan Jones, 'Get Real. Terry Pratchett is Not a Literary Genius', *The Guardian*, 31 August 2015, https://www.theguardian.com/artanddesign/jonathanjonesblog/2015/aug/31/terry-pratchett-is-not-a-literary-genius (accessed 2 October 2025); Jonathan Jones, 'I've Read Pratchett Now: It's More Entertainment Than Art', *The Guardian*, 11 September 2015; A. S. Byatt, 'The Shepherd's Crown by Terry Pratchett Review: The Much-loved Author's Last Discworld Novel', *The Guardian*, 27 August 2015, https://www.theguardian.com/books/2015/aug/27/the-shepherds-crown-terry-pratchett-review-discworld (accessed 2 October 2025); Sam Jordison, 'Terry Pratchett's Books are the Opposite of "Ordinary Potboilers"', *The Guardian*, 31 August 2015, https://www.theguardian.com/books/

booksblog/2015/aug/31/terry-pratchett-opposite-of-ordinary-potboiler-jonathan-jones (accessed 2 October 2025).

9 Andrew M. Butler, Edward James and Farah Mendlesohn (eds), *Terry Pratchett: Guilty of Literature* (Reading: The Science Fiction Foundation, 2000: rev. and expanded, Baltimore: Old Earth Books, 2004).

10 Andrew M. Butler, *Terry Pratchett* (Harpenden: Pocket Essentials, 2001); Andrew Butler (ed.), *An Unofficial Companion to the Novels of Terry Pratchett* (Oxford/Westport, CT: Greenwood World Publishing, 2007); Lawrence Watt-Evans, *The Turtle Moves!* (Dallas, TX, Benbella Books, 2008).

11 Jacob Held and James South (eds), *Philosophy and Terry Pratchett* (Basingstoke: Palgrave Macmillan, 2014); Anne Hiebert Alton, William C. Spruiell, Donald E. Palumbo and C. W. Sullivan III (eds), *Discworld and the Disciplines: Critical Approaches to the Terry Pratchett Works* (Jefferson, NC: McFarland, 2014); Nicolas Michaud (ed.), *Discworld and Philosophy: Reality Is Not What It Seems* (Chicago: Open Court, 2016); Marion Rana, *Terry Pratchett's Narrative Worlds* (Cham: Palgrave, 2018); Justine Breton, *Power and Society in Terry Pratchett's Discworld: Building a Fantasy Civilization* (London: Bloomsbury, 2025).

12 Rebecca Ann Bach, *Terry Pratchett Could Save the World* (New York: Routledge, 2023).

13 Wilkins, *Terry Pratchett*, 372.

2. THE EARLY WORKS

1 *Science Fantasy*, vol. 20, no. 60 (1963), 66.

2 Edward James, 'Weaving the Carpet', in Butler, James and Mendlesohn (eds), *Terry Pratchett: Guilty of Literature*, 40.

3 John Clute, 'Coming of Age', in Butler, James and Mendlesohn (eds), *Terry Pratchett: Guilty of Literature*, 22.

4 Wilkins, *Terry Pratchett*, 191.

5 Qtd in Wilkins, *Terry Pratchett*, 193.

6 Péter Hajdu, 'Terry Pratchett's "China" in *Interesting Times'*, *Neohelicon* 52 (2025), 91–100. Hajdu also notes that the 2008 television adaptation of *The Colour of Magic* portrays Twoflower as 'a stereotypical American tourist wearing shorts and very colourful shirts' (93).

7 Fritz Leiber, *Two Sought Adventure* (New York: Gnome Press, 1957), 5. Pratchett would almost certainly have come across this 'Induction' reprinted in the paperback editions of *Swords and Deviltry* (Ace, 1970; New English Library, 1971).

8 Robert E. Howard, 'The Phoenix on the Sword', *Weird Tales* 20:6 (Dec. 1932), 769. The popular 'Conan' stories were republished by Lancer (USA) and Sphere (UK) during the 60s and 70s. 'The Phoenix on the Sword' appeared also in the *Skull-Face Omnibus* (Neville Spearman, 1974) which would have been found in many libraries, while the epigraph to 'Phoenix' became a kind of separate introduction to the Conan saga.

9 'The Colour of Magic', *lspace.org*, https://www.lspace.org/books/apf/the-colour-of-magic.html (accessed 7 December 2024).

10 Barbara Davis, 'Equal Rites' [review], *Vector* 135 (April/May 1987), 121.

11 George MacDonald, 'The Fantastic Imagination', in *A Dish of Orts* (London: Sampson, Low, Marston, 1895), 314; J. R. R. Tolkien, 'On Fairy-stories', in *Tree and Leaf* (London: Unwin, 1972), 25.

12 Diana Wynne Jones, *Tough Guide to Fantasyland* (London: Vista, 1996).

13 Farah Mendlesohn and Edward James, *A Short History of Fantasy* (London: Middlesex University Press, 2009), 179.

14 Tom Hutchinson, 'Galactic Giggle', *The Times*, 9 June 1988, 19.

15 Penny Hill, 'Unseen University', in Butler, James and Mendlesohn (eds), *Terry Pratchett: Guilty of Literature*, 95.

3. MAPPING DISCWORLD

1 Terry Pratchett (with Jaqueline Simpson), *The Folklore of Discworld* (London: Doubleday, 2008), 147–150.

2 Stacie Hanes, 'Weatherwax, Granny Esmerelda', in Butler (ed.), *An Unofficial Companion*, 408.

3 Terry Pratchett, *The Art of Discworld* (with Paul Kidby) (London: Gollancz, 2004).

4 Cory Doctorow, 'A Conversation with Terry Pratchett', *Boing Boing*, 5 November 2013, https://boingboing.net/2013/11/05/a-conversation-with-terry-prat.html (accessed 7 December 2024).

5 Wilkins, *Terry Pratchett*, 411.

6 Wilkins, *Terry Pratchett*, 419.

7 Edward James, 'The City Watch', in Butler, James and Mendlesohn (eds), *Terry Pratchett: Guilty of Literature*, 193–194.

8 Wilkins, *Terry Pratchett*, 300.

9 James Brown, 'Believing is Seeing: Silas Tomkyn Comberbache and Terry Pratchett', in Butler, James and Mendlesohn (eds), *Terry Pratchett: Guilty of Literature*, 288.

10 James Brown, 'Believing is Seeing', in Butler, James and Mendlesohn (eds), *Terry Pratchett: Guilty of Literature*, 291.

11　Steven H. Silver, 'An Interview with Terry Pratchett', *SF Site*, https://www.stevenhsilver.com/ivtp.html (accessed 1 February 2026).

12　Stacie Hanes, 'Death and the Maiden', in Butler, James and Mendlesohn (eds), *Terry Pratchett: Guilty of Literature*, 181.

13　Nickianne Moody, 'Death and Work', in Butler, James and Mendlesohn (eds), *Terry Pratchett: Guilty of Literature*, 153–170; Bach, Terry Pratchett Could Save the World, 99–120.

14　Moody, 'Death and Work', in Butler, James and Mendlesohn (eds), *Terry Pratchett: Guilty of Literature*, 160–161.

15　Bach, *Terry Pratchett Could Save the World*, 105.

16　Charles Fort, [1931], *Lo!* (New York: Ace, 1973), 20.

17　Martin Brown, 'Imaginary Places Real Monuments: Field Monuments of Lancre, Terry Pratchett's Discworld', in Russell, Miles (ed.), *Digging Holes in Popular Culture* (Oxford: Oxbow Books, 2002), 75.

18　Brown, 'Imaginary Places', 72; Pratchett and Simpson, *Folklore*, 184–187.

19　Brown, 'Imaginary Places', 68–70; Pratchett and Simpson, *Folklore*, 179.

20　Wilkins, *Terry Pratchett*, 427.

21　Watt-Evans, *The Turtle Moves!*, 196.

4. OUTSIDE DISCWORLD: THE NON-SERIES WORKS

1　Wilkins, *Terry Pratchett*, 229.

2　Pratchett's account is cited online in the Annotated Pratchett File, https://www.lspace.org/books/apf/good-omens.html (accessed 3 October 2025).

3　Wilkins, *Terry Pratchett*, 235.

4　John Clute and David Langford, 'Pocket Universe', in *The Encyclopedia of Science Fiction*, https://sf-encyclopedia.com/entry/pocket_universe (accessed 15 December 2024).

5　Peter Hunt, 'Terry Pratchett', in Hunt, Peter, and Millicent Lenz, *Alternative Worlds in Fantasy Fiction* (London: Bloomsbury, 2005), 99–100.

6　Hunt, 'Terry Pratchett', 106, 113.

7　Cherith Baldry, 'The Children's Books', in Butler, James and Mendlesohn (eds), *Terry Pratchett: Guilty of Literature*, 60.

8　Maria Błaszkiewicz, '"You Turn Worlds Upside Down": The Politics of Reversal in Terry Pratchett's Nation', in Le Juez, Brigitte and Olga Springer (eds), *Shipwreck and Island Motifs in Literature and the Arts* (Berlin: Brill, 2015), 273.

9　Pratchett, *Keyboard*, 173.

5. PRATCHETT AND THE 'CAULDRON OF STORY'

1   Tolkien, 'On Fairy-stories', 29.
2   Andrew Gordon, 'Star Wars: A Myth for Our Time', *Literature/Film Quarterly* 6:4 (Fall 1978), 314–326.
3   Tolkien, *Tree and Leaf*, 31.
4   John Clute, 'Cauldron of Story' and 'Ocean of Story', in Clute, John and John Grant (eds), *The Encyclopedia of Fantasy* (London: Orbit, 1997), 174, 704.
5   Tolkien, 'On Fairy Stories', 22; 29–30.
6   Fredric Jameson, 'Magical Narratives: Romance as Genre', *New Literary History* 7:1 (Autumn 1975), 135.
7   Edward James and Farah Mendlesohn (eds), *The Cambridge Companion to Science Fiction* (Cambridge: Cambridge University Press, 2003), 5.
8   Farah Mendlesohn, *Rhetorics of Fantasy* (Middletown, CT: Wesleyan University Press, 2008), 99–100.
9   Damon Knight, *In Search of Wonder* (Chicago: Advent, 1967), 1.
10 Alan Garner, 'Inner Time', in Nicholls, Peter (ed.), *Explorations of the Marvellous* (London: Fontana, 1978), 119–140; Sarah Beach, 'Breaking the Pattern: Alan Garner's *The Owl Service and The Mabinogion*', *Mythlore* 20:1 (Winter 1994), 10–14.
11 Alexandra Rehfeld, Jan Schnitker and Matthias Schroder, 'Fantasy is the Whole Cake: An Interview with Terry Pratchett', in Freiburg, Rudolf and Jan Schnitker (eds), *'Do You Consider Yourself a Postmodern Author?': Interviews with Contemporary English Writers* (Münster: Lit Verlag, 2000), 183.
12 Rehfeld et al., 'Fantasy is the Whole Cake', 183, 189.
13 'Words from the Master', https://www.lspace.org/books/apf/words-from-the-master.html (accessed 12 December 2024).
14 For more on Arabella Buckley, see Melanie Keene, *Science in Wonderland* (Oxford: Oxford University Press, 2015).
15 Kevin Paul Smith, *The Postmodern Fairytale: Folkloric Intertexts in Contemporary Fiction* (Basingstoke: Palgrave Macmillan, 2007), 9.
16 Smith, *Postmodern Fairytale*, 133.
17 Rehfeld et al., 'Fantasy is the Whole Cake', 180.
18 J. R. R. Tolkien, [1955], *The Return of the King* (London: Unwin, 1974), 326.
19 Rehfeld et al., 'Fantasy is the Whole Cake', 189; https://www.lspace.org/books/apf/words-from-the-master.html (accessed 12 December 2024).
20 David Langford, 'Introduction', in Butler, James and Mendlesohn (eds), *Terry Pratchett: Guilty of Literature*, 11.

21 Aleksander Rzyman, *The Intertextuality of Terry Pratchett's Discworld as a Major Challenge for the Translator* (Newcastle Upon Tyne: Cambridge Scholars, 2017).

22 Rzyman, *Intertextuality*, 101.

23 Andrew M. Butler, 'Theories of Humour', in Butler, James and Mendlesohn (eds), *Terry Pratchett: Guilty of Literature*, 83–88.

24 Hajdu, 'Terry Pratchett's "China"', 92.

25 Hajdu, 'Terry Pratchett's "China"', 92.

26 Hajdu, 'Terry Pratchett's "China"', 99.

27 Mendlesohn, *Rhetorics*, 99.

28 Edward James, 'The City Watch', in Butler, James and Mendlesohn (eds), *Terry Pratchett: Guilty of Literature*, 193–216.

29 Mendlesohn, *Rhetorics*, 91.

30 Mendlesohn, *Rhetorics*, 91.

31 Ed McBain, [1956], *The Mugger* (New York: Dell, 1969).

32 Jack Cohen and Ian Stewart, *The Collapse of Chaos* (London: Penguin, 1995), 10.

33 Smith, *Postmodern Fairytale*, 144–147.

34 Karen Sayer, 'The Witches', in Butler, James and Mendlesohn (eds), *Terry Pratchett: Guilty of Literature*, 149.

35 Rehfeld, 'Fantasy is the Whole Cake', 181.

6. FANTASY OR SCIENCE FICTION?

1 Ian Stewart, 'Mathematics, the Media, and the Public', *Proceedings of the International Congress of Mathematicians* (Madrid, Spain, 2006), 1643.

2 Fort, *Lo!*, 20.

3 Arthur C. Clarke, *Profiles of the Future* (London: Gollancz, 1999), 2.

7. MORALITY AND ETHICS

1 John Newsinger, 'The People's Republic of Treacle Mine Road Betrayed: Terry Pratchett's *Night Watch*', *Vector* 232 (November/December 2003), 16.

2 Eve Smith, 'Civil Discobedience or War, Terrorism and Unrest in Terry Pratchett's Discworld', *Comedy Studies* 3:1 (2012), 30, 31; Helena Esser, 'Freedom! Truth! And Justice! in The Big Wahoonie: Ankh-Morpork's neo-Victorian Urbanity', in Breton (ed.), *Power and Society in Terry Pratchett's Discworld: Building a Fantasy Civilization*, 55.

3 Interview with Terry Pratchett, FTL (March 2005), https://www.

oocities.org/fasterthanlife_2000/int_pratchard.htm (accessed 4 December 2024).

4 Victoria Martin, 'Analysis: In Defence of Niceness', *Discworld Chronicle* 2 (1997), 12.

5 Janet Brennan Croft, 'Nice, Good, or Right: Faces of the Wise Woman in Terry Pratchett's "Witches" Novels', *Mythlore* 26:3 (2008), 151–164.

6 Croft, 'Nice, Good, or Right', 157.

7 Croft, 'Nice, Good, or Right', 161.

8 Martin, 'Niceness', 13.

9 Croft, 'Nice, Good, or Right', 161.

10 Farah Mendleson, 'Faith and Ethics', in Butler, James and Mendlesohn (eds), *Terry Pratchett: Guilty of Literature*, 239–260.

11 Mendleson, 'Faith and Ethics', 251.

12 Mendleson, 'Faith and Ethics', 252.

13 Bach, *Terry Pratchett Could Save the World*, 85.

14 von Czarnowsky, 'Editorial', *Gender Studies*, 5.

15 Jacob M. Held, 'A Golem is Not Born, but Rather Becomes, a Woman: Gender on the Disc', in Held and South (eds), *Philosophy and Terry Pratchett*, 7–9, 16–17.

16 Katherine Lashley, 'Monstrous Women: Feminism in Terry Pratchett's Monstrous Regiment', *Gender Forum* 52 (2015), 34.

17 'Our Patrons', Humanists UK, https://humanists.uk/about/our-people/patrons/terry-pratchett/ (accessed 4 December 2024).

8. PRATCHETT AND HIS AUDIENCES

1 Terry Pratchett (@terryandrob), 'AT LAST, SIR TERRY, WE MUST WALK TOGETHER.', Twitter (now X), 12 March 2015, https://x.com/terryandrob/status/576036599047258112?lang=en.

2 Rehfeld, 'Fantasy is the Whole Cake', 189, 188.

3 Wilkins, *Terry Pratchett*, 82.

4 Wilkins, *Terry Pratchett*, 231; Christopher Priest, 'A Middlebrow Cult', *Times Literary Supplement*, 28 October 2022, 18–19.

5 Paul Kincaid, 'Terry Pratchett', *Times Literary Supplement*, 11 November 2022, 6.

6 Jakob Löfgren, '"It's a Good Job Nobody Mentioned Hedgehogs": The Use of Narratives in Discworld Fandom', *Folklore* 128 (March 2017), 75–92.

7 Wilkins, *Terry Pratchett*, 277.

8 Wilkins, *Terry Pratchett*, 195.

9 Eve Smith, 'Engaging with Comedy as Social Conscience in Terry Pratchett's "Discworld"', Doctoral thesis, Liverpool John Moores University, 2016, 227.

10 Tansy Rayner Roberts, *Pratchett's Women: Unauthorised Essays on Female Characters of the Discworld*, 2nd edition (Kindle, 2022), 2.

11 Roberts, *Pratchett's Women*, 3.

12 Roberts, *Pratchett's Women*, 28.

13 Roberts, *Pratchett's Women*, 82–83.

14 Roberts, *Pratchett's Women*, 48.

15 Roberts, *Pratchett's Women*, 3.

16 Anne Heibert Alton, 'Coloring in Octarine: Visual Semiotics and Discworld', in Alton, Spruiell, Palumbo and Sullivan (eds), *Discworld and the Disciplines: Critical Approaches to the Terry Pratchett Works*, 31.

17 Alton, 'Colouring in Octarine', 32.

18 Byatt, 'Foreword' to Terry Pratchett, *A Blink of the Screen*, 11.

19 Alton, 'Colouring in Octarine', 32.

20 Alton, 'Colouring in Octarine', 67; Paul Kidby, *Designing Terry Pratchett's Discworld* (London: Doubleday, 2024), 20.

21 Eve Smith's 'Engaging with Comedy' research was confined to people over 16. But her readership demography shows age ranges of 16–25 (22%), 26–35 (30%) and 36–45 (23%); Smith, 'Engaging with Comedy', 27.

22 Ben Saunders, 'Equality and Difference: Just Because the Disc is Flat, Doesn't Make it a Level Playing Field for All', in Held and South (eds), *Philosophy and Terry Pratchett*, 157–176.

23 William Barnett, 'Review: Terry Pratchett: Guilty of Literature', *Discworld Monthly* 39 (July 2000), https://betterthanapokeintheeye.co.uk/dwarchive/issue0039#S_10 (accessed 5 October 2025); Richard Dansky, 'Andrew M. Butler, Edward James and Farah Mendlesohn's Terry Pratchett: Guilty of Literature', https://agreenmanreview.com/books/andrew-m-butler-edward-james-and-farah-mendlesohns-terry-pratchett-guilty-of-literature/ (accessed 5 October 2025).

24 John Mullan, 'The Triumph of Fantasy Fiction', *The Guardian*, 3 April 2015, https://www.theguardian.com/books/2015/apr/03/george-rr-martin-game-of-thrones-and-the-triumph-of-fantasy-fiction (accessed 5 December 2024); Maureen Kincaid Speller, 'We Need To Talk About Dragons – John Mullan, George RR Martin, Game of Thrones and the Triumph of Fantasy Fiction', https://paperknife.wordpress.com/2015/04/10/we-need-to-talk-about-dragons-john-mullan-george-rr-martin-game-of-thrones-and-the-triumph-of-fantasy-fiction (accessed 5 December 2024).

25 Burrows, *Magic of Terry Pratchett*, 220.

26 Alton, 'Colouring in Octarine', 75, 54.

Selected Bibliography

TERRY PRATCHETT BIBLIOGRAPHY

Terry Pratchett wrote forty-one Discworld novels. Many of these were repackaged in omnibus or collectors' editions, adapted as graphic novels or play-texts, or formed the basis of associated texts such as the Diaries, Handbooks and Almanacs, and maps produced in collaboration with Stephen Briggs and others. Pratchett also provided text for art collections and approved text for a series of Discworld Companions (1994–2021) compiled by Stephen Briggs. In addition, he wrote other novels for adults and children, many of which in their turn have been repackaged. This select bibliography is of primary texts and omits most of the associated works which, however, are important for a fuller appreciation of Pratchett's work and its impact upon his audience. Readers are therefore directed to the website maintained by Pratchett's former agent Colin Smythe at https://colinsmythe.co.uk/terry-pratchett/.

DISCWORLD NOVELS

The Colour of Magic (Gerrards Cross: Colin Smythe, 1983).
The Light Fantastic (Gerrards Cross: Colin Smythe, 1986).
Equal Rites (London: Gollancz/Colin Smythe, 1987).
Mort (London: Gollancz/Colin Smythe, 1987).
Sourcery (London: Gollancz/Colin Smythe, 1988).
Wyrd Sisters (London: Gollancz, 1988).
Pyramids (London: Gollancz, 1989).

Guards! Guards! (London: Gollancz, 1989).
Eric (London: Gollancz, 1990).
Moving Pictures (London: Gollancz, 1990).
Reaper Man (London: Gollancz, 1991).
Witches Abroad (London: Gollancz, 1991).
Small Gods (London: Gollancz, 1992).
Lords and Ladies (London: Gollancz, 1992).
Men at Arms (London: Gollancz, 1993).
Soul Music (London: Gollancz, 1994).
Interesting Times (London: Gollancz, 1994).
Maskerade (London: Gollancz, 1995).
Feet of Clay (London: Gollancz, 1996).
Hogfather (London: Gollancz, 1996).
Jingo (London: Gollancz, 1997).
The Last Continent (London: Doubleday, 1998).
Carpe Jugulum (London: Doubleday, 1998).
The Fifth Elephant (Doubleday, 1999).
The Truth (London: Doubleday, 2000).
Thief of Time (London: Doubleday, 2001).
The Last Hero (London: Gollancz, 2001).
The Amazing Maurice and his Educated Rodents (London: Doubleday, 2001).
Night Watch (London: Doubleday, 2002).
The Wee Free Men (London: Doubleday, 2003).
Monstrous Regiment (London: Doubleday, 2003).
A Hat Full of Sky (London: Doubleday, 2004).
Going Postal (London: Doubleday, 2004).
Thud! (London: Doubleday, 2005).
Wintersmith (London: Doubleday, 2006).
Making Money (London: Doubleday, 2007).
Unseen Academicals (London: Doubleday, 2009).
I Shall Wear Midnight (London: Doubleday, 2010).
Snuff (London: Doubleday, 2011).
Raising Steam (London: Doubleday, 2013).
The Shepherd's Crown (London: Doubleday, 2015).

SCIENCE OF DISCWORLD

The Science of Discworld (with Ian Stewart and Jack Cohen) (London: Ebury Press, 1999; updated 2002).
The Science of Discworld II: the Globe (with Ian Stewart and Jack Cohen) (London: Ebury Press 2002).
The Science of Discworld III: Darwin's Watch (with Ian Stewart and Jack Cohen) (London: Ebury Press, 2005).

The Science of Discworld IV: Judgement Day (with Ian Stewart and Jack Cohen) (London: Ebury Press, 2013).

ASSOCIATED

The Pratchett Portfolio A Compendium of Discworld Characters (with Paul Kidby) (London: Gollancz, 1996).
The Art of Discworld (with Paul Kidby) (London: Gollancz, 2004).
Where's My Cow? (London: Doubleday, 2005).
The Folklore of Discworld (with Jacqueline Simpson) (London Doubleday, 2008).
The World of Poo (London: Doubleday, 2012).
Dodger's Guide to London (London: Doubleday, 2013).

Non-Discworld
The Carpet People (Gerrards Cross: Colin Smythe, 1971).
The Dark Side of the Sun (Gerrards Cross: Colin Smythe, 1976).
Strata (Gerrards Cross: Colin Smythe, 1981).
Truckers (London: Doubleday, 1989).
The Unadulterated Cat (with Gray Jolliffe) (London: Gollancz, 1989).
Good Omens (with Neil Gaiman) (London: Gollancz, 1990).
Diggers (London: Doubleday, 1990).
Wings (London: Doubleday, 1990).
The Carpet People [revised edition] (London: Doubleday, 1992).
Only You Can Save Mankind (London: Doubleday, 1992).
Johnny and the Dead (London: Doubleday, 1993).
Johnny and the Bomb (London: Doubleday, 1996).
Nation (London: Doubleday, 2008).
Dodger (London: Doubleday, 2012).

THE LONG EARTH SERIES (CO-WRITTEN WITH STEPHEN BAXTER)

The Long Earth (London: Doubleday, 2012).
The Long War (London: Doubleday, 2013).
The Long Mars (London: Doubleday, 2014).
The Long Utopia (London: Doubleday, 2015).
The Long Cosmos (London: Doubleday, 2016).

COLLECTIONS

Once More with Footnotes (Framingham, Mass: NESFA Press, 2004).
A Blink of the Screen (London: Doubleday, 2012).
A Slip of the Keyboard (London: Doubleday, 2014).
Dragons at Crumbling Castle (London: Doubleday, 2014).
The Witch's Vacuum Cleaner (London: Doubleday, 2016).
Father Christmas's Fake Beard (London: Doubleday, 2017).
The Time-Travelling Caveman (London: Doubleday, 2020).
A Stroke of the Pen: The Lost Stories (London: HarperCollins, 2023).

SELECTED INTERVIEWS WITH/ESSAYS BY PRATCHETT

[Anon], Interview with Terry Pratchett, *FTL* (March 2005), https://www.oocities.org/fasterthanlife_2000/int_pratchard.htm (accessed 4 December 2024).
Pratchett, Terry, 'Imaginary Worlds, Real Stories', *Folklore* 111:2 (Oct. 2000), 159–168.
Pratchett, Terry, 'Terry Pratchett's 2009 Boston Globe-Horn Book Fiction Award Speech for Nation', *Horn Book*, 12 March 2015, https://www.hbook.com/story/terry-pratchetts-2009-boston-globe-horn-book-fiction-award-speech-for-nation (accessed 15 October 2024).
Pratchett, Terry, 'Words from the Master', https://www.lspace.org/books/apf/words-from-the-master.html (accessed 12 December 2024).
Rehfeld, Alexandra, Jan Schnitker and Mattias Schröder, 'Fantasy is the Whole Cake: An Interview with Terry Pratchett', in Freiburg, Rudolf and Jan Schnitker (eds), *'Do You Consider Yourself a Postmodern Author?': Interviews with Contemporary English Writers* (Munster: Lit Verlag, 2000), 179–199.
Silver, Steven H., 'An Interview with Terry Pratchett', *SF Site*, https://www.sfsite.com/04b/tp79.htm (accessed 7 December 2024).

SELECTED CRITICAL BIBLIOGRAPHY

Alton, Anne Hiebert, William C. Spruiell, Donald E. Palumbo and C. W. Sullivan III (eds), *Discworld and the Disciplines: Critical Approaches to the Terry Pratchett Works* (Jefferson, NC: McFarland, 2014).
Bach, Rebecca Ann, *Terry Pratchett Could Save the World* (New York: Routledge, 2023).

Barnett, William, 'Review: Terry Pratchett: Guilty of Literature', *Discworld Monthly* 39 (July 2000), https://betterthanapokeintheeye. co.uk/dwarchive/issue0039#S_10 (accessed 5 October 2025).

Beach, Sarah, 'Breaking the Pattern: Alan Garner's *The Owl Service* and *The Mabinogion*', *Mythlore* 20:1 (75) (Winter 1994), 10–14.

Błaszkiewicz, Maria, '"You Turn Worlds Upside Down": The Politics of Reversal in Terry Pratchett's *Nation*', in Le Juez, Brigitte and Olga Springer (eds), *Shipwreck and Island Motifs in Literature and the Arts* (Berlin: Brill, 2015), 267–280.

Breton, Justine (ed.), *Power and Society in Terry Pratchett's Discworld: Building a Fantasy Civilization* (London: Bloomsbury, 2025).

Brown, Martin, 'Imaginary Places Real Monuments: Field Monuments of Lancre, Terry Pratchett's Discworld', in Russell, Miles (ed.), *Digging Holes in Popular Culture* (Oxford: Oxbow Books, 2002), 67–76.

Burrows, Marc, *The Magic of Terry Pratchett* (Barnsley: Pen & Sword, 2020).

Butler, Andrew M., *Terry Pratchett* (Harpenden: Pocket Essentials, 2001).

Butler, Andrew (ed.), *An Unofficial Companion to the Novels of Terry Pratchett* (Oxford/Westport, CT: Greenwood World Publishing, 2007).

Butler, Andrew M., Edward James and Farah Mendlesohn (eds), *Terry Pratchett: Guilty of Literature* (Reading: The Science Fiction Foundation, 2000: rev. and expanded, Baltimore: Old Earth Books, 2004).

Byatt, A. S., '*The Shepherd's Crown* by Terry Pratchett Review: The Much-loved Author's Last Discworld Novel', *The Guardian*, 27 August 2015, https://www.theguardian.com/books/2015/aug/27/ the-shepherds-crown-terry-pratchett-review-discworld (accessed 2 October 2025).

Cabell, Craig, *Terry Pratchett: The Spirit of Fantasy* (London: John Blake, 2011).

Clarke, Arthur C., *Profiles of the Future* (London: Gollancz, 1999).

Clute, John and David Langford, 'Pocket Universe', in *The Encyclopedia of Science Fiction*, https://sf-encyclopedia.com/entry/pocket_universe (accessed 15 December 2024).

Clute, John and John Grant (eds), *The Encyclopedia of Fantasy* (London: Orbit, 1997).

Cohen, Jack and Ian Stewart, *The Collapse of Chaos* (London: Penguin, 1995).

Croft, Janet Brennan, 'Nice, Good, or Right: Faces of the Wise Woman in Terry Pratchett's "Witches" Novels', *Mythlore* 26:3 (2008), 151–164.

Dansky, Richard, 'Andrew M. Butler, Edward James and Farah Mendlesohn's Terry Pratchett: Guilty of Literature', https:// agreenmanreview.com/books/andrew-m-butler-edward-james-and-farah-mendlesohns-terry-pratchett-guilty-of-literature/ (accessed 5 October 2025).

Davis, Barbara, 'Equal Rites' [review], *Vector* 135 (April/May 1987), 121.

Doctorow, Cory, 'A Conversation with Terry Pratchett', *Boing Boing*, 5 November 2013, https://boingboing.net/2013/11/05/a-conversation-with-terry-prat.html (accessed 7 December 2024).

Fort, Charles, [1931], *Lo!* (New York, Ace, 1973).

Garner, Alan, 'Inner Time', in Nicholls, Peter (ed.), *Explorations of the Marvellous* (London: Fontana, 1978), 119–140.

Garry, Jane and Hasan El-Shamy (eds), *Archetypes and Motifs in Folklore and Literature: A Handbook* (London: Routledge, 2016).

Gordon, Andrew, 'Star Wars: A Myth for Our Time', *Literature/Film Quarterly* 6:4 (Fall 1978), 314–326.

Hajdu, Péter, 'Terry Pratchett's "China" in *Interesting Times*', *Neohelicon* 52 (2025), 91–100.

Hanes, Stacie, 'The Nineteenth-Century Foundations of the Discworld, or, More Than You Needed to Know About Granny Weatherwax's Knickers', *New York Review of Science Fiction* (July 2009), 11–12.

Held, Jacob and James South (eds), *Philosophy and Terry Pratchett* (Basingstoke: Palgrave Macmillan, 2014).

Howard, Robert E., 'The Phoenix on the Sword', *Weird Tales* 20:6 (Dec. 1932), 769–784.

Hunt, Peter, 'Terry Pratchett', in Hunt, Peter and Millicent Lenz, *Alternative Worlds in Fantasy Fiction* (London: Bloomsbury, 2005), 86–121.

Hutchinson, Tom, 'Galactic Giggle', *The Times*, 9 June 1988, 19.

James, Edward and Farah Mendlesohn (eds), *The Cambridge Companion to Science Fiction* (Cambridge: Cambridge University Press, 2003).

Jameson, Fredric, 'Magical Narratives: Romance as Genre', *New Literary History* 7:1 (Autumn 1975), 135–163.

Johnson, Boris, 'Rich Imagination of Discworld's Doyen', *Daily Telegraph*, 11 May 1998, 34.

Jones, Diana Wynne, *The Tough Guide to Fantasyland* (London: Vista, 1996).

Jones, Jonathan, 'Get Real. Terry Pratchett is Not a Literary Genius', *The Guardian*, 31 August 2015, https://www.theguardian.com/artanddesign/jonathanjonesblog/2015/aug/31/terry-pratchett-is-not-a-literary-genius (accessed 2 October 2025).

Jones, Jonathan, 'I've Read Pratchett Now: It's More Entertainment Than Art', *The Guardian*, 11 September 2015, https://www.theguardian.com/artanddesign/jonathanjonesblog/2015/sep/11/jonathan-jones-ive-read-terry-pratchett-now-its-more-entertainment-than-art (accessed 2 October 2025).

Jordison, Sam, 'Terry Pratchett's Books are the Opposite of "Ordinary Potboilers"', *The Guardian*, 31 August 2015, https://www.theguardian.com/books/booksblog/2015/aug/31/terry-pratchett-opposite-of-ordinary-potboiler-jonathan-jones (accessed 2 October 2025).

Kidby, Paul, *Designing Terry Pratchett's Discworld* (London: Doubleday, 2024).

Kincaid, Paul, 'Terry Pratchett', *Times Literary Supplement*, 11 November 2022, 6.

Knight, Damon, *In Search of Wonder* (Chicago: Advent, 1967).

Lashley, Katherine, 'Monstrous Women: Feminism in Terry Pratchett's *Monstrous Regiment*', *Gender Forum* 52 (2015), 26–38.

Leiber, Fritz, *Two Sought Adventure* (New York: Gnome Press, 1957).

Löfgren, Jakob, '"It's a Good Job Nobody Mentioned Hedgehogs": The Use of Narratives in Discworld Fandom', *Folklore* 128 (March 2017), 75–92.

MacDonald, George, 'The Fantastic Imagination', in *A Dish of Orts* (London: Sampson, Low, Marston, 1895), 313–322.

Martin, Victoria, 'Analysis: In Defence of Niceness', *Discworld Chronicle* 2 (1997), 12–13.

Martin, Victoria, 'Analysis: The Dangers of Goodness', *Discworld Chronicle* 4 (1998), 22–23.

McBain, Ed, [1956], *The Mugger* (New York: Dell, 1969).

McMurry, Margarida, 'Story Matters: Story and Its Concept in Tolkien and Pratchett', in Schmeink, Lars and Astrid Böge (eds), *Collision of Realities: Establishing Research on the Fantastic in Europe* (Berlin: Walter de Gruyter, 2012).

Mendlesohn, Farah, *Rhetorics of Fantasy* (Middletown, CT: Wesleyan University Press, 2008).

Mendlesohn, Farah, 'Writing a Ruritania in a Post Colonialist World', *Vector* 263 (Summer 2010), 11–15.

Mendlesohn, Farah and Edward James, *A Short History of Fantasy* (London: Middlesex University Press, 2009).

Michaud, Nicolas (ed.), *Discworld and Philosophy: Reality Is Not What It Seems* (Chicago: Open Court, 2016).

Mullan, John, 'The Triumph of Fantasy Fiction', *The Guardian*, 3 April 2015, https://www.theguardian.com/books/2015/apr/03/george-rr-martin-game-of-thrones-and-the-triumph-of-fantasy-fiction (accessed 5 December 2024).

Newsinger, John, 'The People's Republic of Treacle Mine Road Betrayed: Terry Pratchett's Night Watch', *Vector* 232 (November/December 2003), 15–16.

Noone, Kristin and Emily Lavin (eds), *Terry Pratchett's Ethical Worlds: Essays on Identity and Narrative in Discworld and Beyond* (Jefferson, NC: McFarland, 2020).

Priest, Christopher, 'A Middlebrow Cult', *Times Literary Supplement*, 28 October 2022, 18–19.

Propp, Vladimir, *Theory and History of Folklore* (Manchester: Manchester University Press, 1984).

Rana, Marion (ed.), *Terry Pratchett's Narrative Worlds: From Giant Turtles to Small Gods* (Cham: Palgrave, 2018).

Roberts, Tansy Rayner, *Pratchett's Women: Unauthorised Essays on Female Characters of the Discworld*, 2nd edition (Kindle, 2022).

Rzyman, Aleksander, *The Intertextuality of Terry Pratchett's Discworld as a Major Challenge for the Translator* (Newcastle Upon Tyne: Cambridge Scholars, 2017).

Santaulària i Capdevila, M. Isabel, 'Age and Rage in Terry Pratchett's "Witches" Novels', *European Journal of English Studies* 22:1 (2018), 59–75.

Sawyer, Andy, 'Narrativium and Lies-to-Children: "Palatable Instruction" in *The Science of Discworld*', *Journal of the Fantastic in the Arts* 13:1 (2003), 62–81.

Sawyer, Andy, 'The Riddle of Medieval Technology' in Kears, Karl and James Paz (eds), *Medieval Science Fiction* (King's College London: Centre for Late Antique & Medieval Studies, 2016), 153–175.

Sinclair, Lian, 'Magical Genders: The Gender(s) of Witches in the Historical Imagination of Terry Pratchett's Discworld', *Mythlore* 126 (Spring/Summer 2015), 7–20.

Smith, Eve, 'Civil Discobedience or War, Terrorism and Unrest in Terry Pratchett's Discworld', *Comedy Studies* 3:1 (2012), 29–39.

Smith, Eve, 'Engaging with Comedy as Social Conscience in Terry Pratchett's "Discworld"', PhD thesis, Liverpool John Moores University, 2016.

Smith, Kevin Paul, *The Postmodern Fairytale: Folkloric Intertexts in Contemporary Fiction* (Basingstoke: Palgrave Macmillan, 2007).

Speller, Maureen Kincaid, 'We Need to Talk About Dragons – John Mullan, George RR Martin, Game of Thrones and the Triumph of Fantasy Fiction', https://paperknife.wordpress.com/2015/04/10/we-need-to-talk-about-dragons-john-mullan-george-rr-martin-game-of-thrones-and-the-triumph-of-fantasy-fiction (accessed 5 December 2024).

Stewart, Ian, 'Mathematics, the Media, and the Public', *Proceedings of the International Congress of Mathematicians*, Vol. 3 (Madrid: European Mathematical Society, 2006), 1632–1644.

Tolkien, J. R. R., 'On Fairy-Stories', in *Tree and Leaf* (London: Unwin, 1972), 11–70.

Tolkien, J. R. R., [1955], *The Return of the King* (London: Unwin, 1974).

von Czarnowsky, Laura-Marie, 'Editorial', *Gender Forum* 52 (2015), 4–5.

Watt-Evans, Lawrence, *The Turtle Moves!* (Dallas, TX: Benbella Books, 2008).

Webb, Caroline, *Fantasy and the Real World in British Children's Literature* (New York and Abingdon: Routledge, 2015).

Wilkins, Rob, *Terry Pratchett: A Life with Footnotes: The Official Biography* (London: Doubleday, 2022).

Index

The manufacturer's authorised representative in the EU for product safety is: Easy Access System Europe, Mustamäe tee 50, 10621 Tallinn, Estonia https://easproject.com (gpsr.requests@easproject.com)